DIVINE COMEDIES

Paul Burbridge
and
Murray Watts

First edition 1994

British Library Cataloguing in Publication Data
A catalogue record for this book is available
from the British Library.

ISBN: 1 85424 276 8

Designed and produced in England for
MONARCH PUBLICATIONS
Broadway House
The Broadway
Crowborough
East Sussex TN6 1HQ by
Nuprint Ltd, Station Road, Harpenden, Herts AL5 4SE.

To the new generation,
to our sons and daughters
and to the members of
the Riding Lights Roughshod companies
who have done so much to continue the original vision
of Riding Lights Theatre Company.

Eee, t'Lord's reet hand teks sum beatin, it duz an all.
Psalm 118 verse 16, in Yorkshire Dialect

Licence to Perform the Sketches In This Volume

mention the title, authors and publishers, in writing if possible.

6. All cassette recording, radio, television, video and film rights are reserved.

Licence applications should be sent to: *Divine Comedies, P.O. Box 223, York, YO1 1GW*. All cheques and money orders should be made out in pounds sterling and made payable to *'Divine Comedies'*.

The above refers to amateur performances (to both paying and non-paying audiences). A separate application should be made to the same address by any professional company wishing to perform this material. Permission will involve the payment of royalties on box-office receipts.

Please note that applications for licences relating to other books of sketches by the same authors should be made on separate cheques made out to the title of the relevant book and sent to the address specified within it.

THE FOREWORD
by Simon Mayo

(The scene is a slightly down-at-heel agency office. A picture of Dave Lee Travis in a gorilla outfit hangs on the wall, next to a framed, crocheted, 'You don't have to be mad to work here, but it helps!' sign. A slightly down-at-heel AGENT, balding and slightly tubby, sits behind a down-at-heel desk. A DJ—young, dashingly handsome and always ready with a merry quip or biblical quote—has just entered)

AGENT   Good to see you, Steve. Sit down.

DJ   It's Simon actually and I'll stand thank you. I recognise a Diddy David Hamilton Collapse-a-Chair when I see one.

AGENT   A number of offers for you, Dave—compère at the Ann Summers convention?

DJ   No thank you.

AGENT   Write a pop column for the Daily Star?

DJ   No thank you.

AGENT   Write the foreword for the new Riding Lights book?

DJ   How much...

AGENT	(*interrupting*) One doesn't do things like this for financial reward.
DJ	No, how much do they want me to do it?
AGENT	Very, very much.
DJ	You're sure they don't really want Adrian Plass?
AGENT	Certainly not.
DJ	Or Cliff?
AGENT	No.
DJ	And not Sheila Walsh?
AGENT	Sheila who?
DJ	Never mind. Well (*flicks through pages*), as they had the wisdom to perform a couple of these sketches on my *Words Into Action* show for *BBC 2*, it's the least I can do. And they're all great actors, profound theologians and personal friends.
AGENT	Really?
DJ	Yes, I met them once at Warwick University in 1977.
AGENT	It's a deal then. Now the Shopping Channel want you to...
	(DJ *walks over to window and opens it. They both freeze*)

INTRODUCTION

Many requests from drama groups and theatre companies far and wide have persuaded us that it is time for a new book of sketches from Riding Lights Theatre Company. It is eight years since the first publication of our last book of material, *Red Letter Days*, and fifteen since our first, *Time to Act*. A new generation of actors has emerged since then. Many of them, if the evidence of those attending our recent Youth Theatre courses in York is anything to go by, are more committed to developing their theatrical skills as Christians and using them to herald the kingdom of God than ever before. This upsurge of creative expression and the encouragement of the increasing numbers of talented Christian performers graduating from our secular drama schools is cause for great hope. It is something which Riding Lights has always tried to foster.

The successful advent over the past two years of our 'younger' Roughshod community companies, training actors and generating new material for use in schools, clubs and colleges, is part of our commitment to the impetus of this new wave. Some of that material has surfaced in this book, which, in itself, will hopefully be another small contribution to the creative flow— releasing a few scripts which you may find useful but, above all, encouraging you to continue to perform live theatre in places where it would not otherwise be experienced. We would also hope to encourage you to continue to be creative, to write your own material and to strive to address the issues and struggles of your own communities.

Theatre will often have that 'Heineken effect', reaching the parts which are inaccessible to other forms of communication; teaching truths that people have forgotten or never heard, raising the spiritual dust but, most importantly, moving people at a level which they sometimes find hard to articulate. Live performance is vital because it brings people together. It counteracts the disintegration experienced by many families and communities, whose lives are overrun by the essential loneliness of armchair entertainment and the inhuman consequences of violence and deprivation. Sketches will, of course, always be the *hors d'oeuvre*, preparing the way for a more substantial theatrical main course, but for many people who wouldn't dream of going to a play, sketches can be the key that opens the door onto a world of imagination, debate and deeper understanding of their situation. Ultimately, we believe that the special relationship between an actor and a theatre audience is a powerful channel for the voice of God, which will never be usurped by the 'cool' communication of film or video. Let us keep theatre *live* and alive.

Ironically, because Riding Lights has concentrated its efforts recently in trying to provide that 'main course', writing and developing full-length productions, many of the sketches reproduced here have been created in response to commissions from other organisations rather than from the needs of our own stage work. The Roughshod output is revitalising our sketch repertoire, but some of these pieces have already become well-known through BBC schools radio and television, from broadcasts on the World Service or through the work of Saltmine, the Church Pastoral Aid Society, and Spring Harvest. However, there is even one curious survivor, a street-theatre puppet script on Daniel, from the very earliest era of our work (with Riding Lights' ancestor Breadrock). This is in sharp contrast with the newest piece, *Power Failure*, which was televised on Maundy Thursday by the BBC this year. But whatever the source, much of this collection has been reworked and sharpened for and by performance on stage.

Divine Comedies includes a broad range of both styles and subjects. There are one or two contributions to that great corpus of material which is voraciously consumed at Christmas and Easter but there are also sketches based on less obvious biblical sources: Pharaoh's dreams, the ten commandments, wisdom literature, the book of Daniel, Philip and the Ethiopian, Mrs Zebedee and so on. There are parables, teaching, even a little theology here and there. In addition to biblical pieces, there are several which touch on 'issues': the environment, materialism, blasphemy, evangelism, prayer or key church topics such as 'giving the notices'. If you are searching for monologues, we have monologues; we have rap, mime, dialogues, duologues, pieces for large casts and small casts, for children, for tricky school assemblies and dodgy RE lessons, real characters and cartoon ones, for good actors and...not-so-good actors...which is all sounding horribly like the blurb on the back of the book but one way or another there should be something here for everyone.

We are delighted to be able to include a couple of sketches by Nigel Forde, who has done so much to establish the style of Riding Lights over the years, and also a couple by Bridget Foreman, a constant creative presence in the early Roughshod companies. We are grateful, too, to Sean Cavanagh, the hub of the company's theatre design, for the visual impact of the cover and to Vicky Wicks and Janis Darrah for their dedicated typing up of the manuscript. Obviously we are also indebted to Dante for suggesting the original idea for the title—though it might be said that his seminal work of European literature, epic as it may be, is somewhat short on jokes.

As a literary form, great comedy (as opposed to the wearisome banalities of television sit-com) is the truest expression of the Christian hope—the triumph of the resurrection and the eternally happy ending of heaven. Great comedy, as Dante understood so well, is profoundly serious. Mankind in defiance of a loving, all-powerful creator is comic, even tragi-comic; men and women in farcical oblivion of the divine story which explains their existence are comic; but the elevation of human beings by the grace of God to partake of eternal glory with Christ is also supremely comic. No wonder Jesus so often described heaven in terms of a party filled with the laughter of celebration. The medieval dramatists, whose plays still endure remarkably well in performance, lived and breathed this view of humanity and the universe. For many of their characters it is the comedy itself which becomes the religious experience; into the comic absurdities of human life, the wonder of the divine bursts through and they are humbled. They kneel in worship, painfully aware of their incongruity, their 'lewdness', in the presence of God. The situation is at once sympathetic, funny and joyous.

Working from York, where some of the finest biblical plays from the middle ages originated, Riding Lights Theatre Company has found inspiration which has strengthened a late twentieth-century flowering of that same tradition. *Divine Comedies* may be a far cry from the grandeur of a Mystery cycle, but the spirit behind it is essentially the same. So is the intention. As in the fourteenth century, many people today have never encountered the Bible in a way they can understand. They need entertaining responses to their questions and those of us who have some gifts in this form of dramatic communication should take more than a leaf out of the methods of Jesus, who was both direct and entertaining at the same time. In the words of the YDV (the Yorkshire Dialect Version), when asked by 'wun on 'em legal eagles i' t'crowd, "Who is ma naabur?", Jesus gizzitim straight an' tells him this yarn'...or possibly, does him this sketch?

Paul Burbridge and Murray Watts
YORK, September 1994

CONTENTS

Life on Plummet Earth

The de-creation story from the Unauthorised Version (Genesis 1–3)

In the beginning God created the heavens and the earth! And God saw everything that he had made and behold it was very good!!

In the end, Man in his wisdom destroyed the heavens and the earth. The earth was without form and void and darkness was upon the face of the deep, for verily an oil-slick the size of Scotland was moving over the face of the waters. And Man said, 'Let there be *Light!*' (*Pause*) And there was no light. So Man cried a second time, saying, 'What we really need is a *light* here, for lo! I cannot see a dicky bird.'

And Man said, 'Let there be an effluent in the midst of the waters.' And it was so. And Man said, 'Let the waters under the effluent be polluted together into one place and let the dry land appear.' And Man called the dry land DESERT and the waters he called UNFIT FOR BATHING. And Man saw that it was vile.

The waters brought forth swarms of living creatures and other bacteria to fill the earth and subdue it. And the birds of the air and the beasts of the earth became creeping things that croaked upon the land. And Man blessed all the substances that he had made, saying, 'Be harmful and multiply.' And it was so.

Thus the heavens and the earth were finished and all the host of them. And the Lord God said unto the Man and the Woman, 'What is this that ye have done? Have ye eaten of the Tree of the Knowledge of Good and Evil, whereof I commanded ye that ye should not eat, lest ye die?' And the Man and the Woman did hum and harr, until the Man did point to the apple, muttering unto the Woman, 'You and your vitamin C!'

The Lord God sent the Man and the Woman forth from the Garden of Eden.

The Hitch-hiker's Guide to the Gospel

NARRATOR 1
NARRATOR 2
PHILIP, the apostle evangelist
ANGEL
The ETHIOPIAN chancellor of the exchequer.

The book of the Acts of the Apostles describes the beginnings of the spread of the gospel of Jesus Christ around the world. Before he ascended into heaven, Jesus charged his disciples to be his witnesses in Jerusalem, Samaria and then moving outwards to the 'uttermost parts of the earth'. The day of Pentecost in Jerusalem, when the Holy Spirit fell on his disciples in great joy and power, was the start of the process. That day alone three thousand Jewish pilgrims from all over the known world responded to the gospel preached by Peter. The book of Acts records the continuing evangelism, spreading out from Jerusalem, as men and women were obedient to the promptings of the Holy Spirit—even if those promptings appeared to be completely mad. This sketch focuses on one of the maddest, but inevitably, one of the most significant examples of personal evangelism in the whole Bible. It encourages us to think of the clubs, the estates, the neighbourhoods, the prisons and the tiny villages on our doorsteps, which for us may represent the 'uttermost parts of the earth' where Jesus has commanded us to be witnesses to him.

(A large map of the world is set centre stage. This features the known world of the New Testament: a huge label saying 'Jerusalem' and very little else. PHILIP *the evangelist enters with two* NARRATORS. *All three are carrying pointing sticks, with which they indicate the relevant geography)*

PHILIP	Now, the history of World Mission
NARRATOR 1	Began in this way.
NARRATOR 2	Firstly, Jesus rose from the dead. Here.
PHILIP	Secondly, Jesus ascended into heaven. Here, or here.

(He points to general area above the map)

NARRATOR 1	Thirdly, the Holy Spirit descended on the disciples. Here.
NARRATOR 2	Fourthly, the Church began to grow. Here.
PHILIP	Initially, things were very much centred on Jerusalem. Er, here.
NARRATOR 1	In fact, very little mission was going on at all.
NARRATOR 2	Here.
PHILIP	Here.
NARRATOR 1	Or here.
NARRATOR 2	All that was to change, of course,
PHILIP	With a little persecution.
NARRATOR 1	A few murderous threats.
NARRATOR 2	Imprisonments
PHILIP	Stonings

23

NARRATOR 1	General ravaging of the church
NARRATOR 2	And so on.
PHILIP	All of this was concentrated, um, here.
NARRATOR 1	In fact, things got so exciting in Jerusalem
	(*They all indicate it*)
PHILIP	That many of the Christians pushed off somewhere else to recover.
NARRATOR 1	Philip,
PHILIP	That's me.
NARRATOR 2	Went off to preach the gospel in Samaria.
PHILIP	Sort of, here.
NARRATOR 1	Where things started to get even more exciting.
NARRATOR 2	Proclaiming the good news!
PHILIP	Miracles!
NARRATOR 1	Exorcisms!
NARRATOR 2	Lots of people coming to the meetings.
PHILIP	Baptisms, healings, cripples walking
NARRATOR 1	Large crowds
NARRATOR 2	At the meetings.
PHILIP	Getting converted! Obeying God! Repenting!
	(*An* ANGEL *has entered and tries to interrupt this wild enthusiasm*)
ANGEL	Philip, hear the word of the Lord...

24

PHILIP	Just a moment. Prayer Meetings! House groups!
NARRATOR 2	Bring-and-share lunches!
NARRATOR 1	Young mums!
ANGEL	Philip!
PHILIP	Hang on a sec. The joy of the Lord! People amazed...!
ANGEL	PHILIP!!!!
	(*They all stop and stare*)
	Can I have a word with you, please?
PHILIP	Certainly. Go and get ready for the meeting, everybody.
	(*The others leave, still repeating mighty acts and developments.* PHILIP *turns to the* ANGEL)
	You're new here aren't you? Tell me, do you know God personally in your life?
ANGEL	Yes. Now look...
PHILIP	It's not enough just to believe in God, you know. We all need to acknowledge Jesus Christ in our hearts as Saviour and Lord.
ANGEL	I know. What I was...
PHILIP	That's wonderful. Well, let's just kneel down and pray a little prayer of commitment here and now. (*He kneels*) I'll pray and you can simply echo these words in your heart.

ANGEL	I am an angel, Philip. An angel of the Lord.
PHILIP	(*Praying*) Lord we thank you for Angel— ah.
	(*Pause*)
	So you've obviously heard about Jesus, then?
ANGEL	I know him well.
PHILIP	Fine. (*Getting up*) Good to have fellowship with you. Would you like to come along to our meeting and share a short testimony? I'm sure that people would love to hear what the Lord's been doing in your life.
ANGEL	I *have* got a message to give as it happens.
PHILIP	We'd love to hear it. I'd got something prepared, obviously, but that's not important. After a couple of songs we could hand straight over...
ANGEL	It's just for you.
PHILIP	That's very kind of you, but I think everyone would be very disappointed...
ANGEL	You've been doing a great job in Samaria,
PHILIP	Well, it was...
ANGEL	So God wants you to go somewhere else.
PHILIP	Why??!

ANGEL	Oh, you're not available?
PHILIP	Technically, of course I'm available, if God...
ANGEL	Here's the message, then. You might want to take this down. God says: 'Go south along the road that runs from Jerusalem to Gaza.'
PHILIP	Yes.
ANGEL	Go south along the road–
PHILIP	From Jerusalem to Gaza. Yes, I've got that. Then what?
ANGEL	That's it.
PHILIP	What do you mean?
ANGEL	That's all it says.
PHILIP	OK, so...er... getting on to that road is obviously the main thing, so...what does God want me to do then?
ANGEL	He didn't say.
PHILIP	Couldn't you give me even a tiny clue?
ANGEL	Sorry.
PHILIP	So am I.

(ANGEL *begins to leave*)

	This is the desert road we're talking about? The one leading into the *desert*. I suppose God is aware of how strategic the work in Samaria really is at the moment, is he?
ANGEL	I detect a certain hesitancy in your attitude to this job.

PHILIP	No, no. I'm very keen, very honoured.
ANGEL	For all you know, it might change the whole course of spreading the gospel.
PHILIP	In the desert, yes.
ANGEL	Or... Africa.
	(ANGEL *leaves*)
PHILIP	(*Laughs*) Africa! Where's that? (*He carries the map off*)
	(*Enter* NARRATOR 1 *shaded by a large golfing umbrella*)
NARRATOR 1	A week later, Philip arrived in the desert.
PHILIP	(*Returning with a handkerchief knotted over his head*) Just as I thought, deserted! Do you want me to start preaching, Lord, and trust that you'll bring someone along? Now listen here, you rocks, I've got some very good news for you.
NARRATOR 1	The sun blazed like a furnace.
	(PHILIP *catches sight of her and gives a great big thumbs-up to God. He approaches the* NARRATOR)
	On either side of the road, sand and rocks stretched to the horizon. Nothing stirred.
PHILIP	Hullo.
NARRATOR 1	(*Puzzled by this interruption*) Hi. Nothing stirred except for the shimmering heat and the occasional lizard.
PHILIP	I am very relieved to find you here. This

is an exciting moment which could change the whole course of spreading the gospel. Tell me, do you know God personally in your life?

NARRATOR 1   (*Whispering*) I'm the Narrator.

PHILIP   (*Whispering back*) God loves you whoever you are.

NARRATOR 1   You don't understand, I'm telling the story.

PHILIP   Oh, I see. Sorry. Carry on.

NARRATOR 1   And then, from the direction of Jerusalem, there, out of the shimmering haze, a handful of dust. Look! A cloud! A bigger cloud!

PHILIP   An enormous cloud!

NARRATOR 1   Horses galloping! A chariot!

(*The other actors enter stage right making hoof noises. Together they suggest a chariot and a horse, of which the wheel is the spinning umbrella, turned by the* NARRATOR. *The* ETHIOPIAN *stands inside engrossed in his reading, nonchalantly holding imaginary reins*)

The Ethiopian Chancellor of the Exchequer!

PHILIP   (*Wild cheering and clapping. He tries to thumb a lift*)

ETHIOPIAN   Wassa matter wid you, man? You wanna lift? Where you going?

PHILIP   I dunno. Where are you going?

ETHIOPIAN	Africa.
PHILIP	Africa!! Tell me, do you know God personally in your life?
	(*He climbs into the chariot*)
ETHIOPIAN	Yessir, I do! Right now, I'm readin' de holy prophets, man. I got dis little book, 'Every day wid Jehovah'.
PHILIP	Doesn't it make you sick?
ETHIOPIAN	(*Outraged*) Dis is de Holy word of God!
PHILIP	I meant, reading in the chariot.
ETHIOPIAN	(*Laughing*) Oh. Doesn't bother me. But I just wish I understood it more.
NARRATOR 1	(*Suddenly sounding like a football commentator*) Oh, yes! he's created the opening! What a fantastic move!
	(*Like a slow-motion clip of a football crowd, rising to celebrate a goal, the chariot dissolves*)
PHILIP	And Philip's there!
ETHIOPIAN	It's in the back of the chariot!
NARRATOR 2	One nil.
	(*Cheering and applause and slow-mo continue*)
NARRATOR 1	He galloped down the road
ETHIOPIAN	Reading the Bible
PHILIP	Totally unmarked
NARRATOR 2	Picked up an evangelist
NARRATOR 1	Created the opening

ETHIOPIAN	And there it was!
PHILIP	The good news of Jesus
NARRATOR 2	And all the way to baptism.
NARRATOR 1	An amazing conversion, Phil.
NARRATOR 2	(*Changing the tone and coming forward*) And the word of God grew.
ETHIOPIAN	Like a flower in the desert
PHILIP	Where you least expect it.
NARRATOR 1	Jerusalem.
PHILIP	Samaria.
ETHIOPIAN	Africa.
NARRATOR 2	The World!
PHILIP	I can see it all!
NARRATOR 1	Where next, Philip? Manila?
ETHIOPIAN	Malawi?
NARRATOR 2	Madrid?
NARRATOR 1	Marseilles?
ETHIOPIAN	Madagascar?
NARRATOR 2	Madras?
PHILIP	(*Very confidently*) Mansfield.
NARRATOR 2	Mansfield??
NARRATOR 1	(*Catching on*) Middlesbrough.
NARRATOR 2	Manchester.
ETHIOPIAN	Maidstone.
NARRATOR 2	Merseyside.

PHILIP   Middle Wallop! (*Or preferably some
              minor but well-known local place begin-
              ning with 'm'*)

NARRATOR 2   Alright, there's no need to get silly
              about it. Come on.

The Christmas Present

Mr LEWIN, a shepherd
SHENKYN, a junior shepherd
DOREEN, Lewin's wife
BRENDA, Shenkyn's wife

For those familiar with our previous book, *Red Letter Days*, this sketch is the 'Further Adventures of Mr Lewin and Shenkyn'. These colourful shepherds (often played as Welsh by Riding Lights) not only appeared in that book but originated in *The Tree That Woke Up* (1975), a full-length Christmas play by Murray Watts. This latest encounter with them was written for a special performance on television to celebrate the twenty-first anniversary of the Arts Centre Group, an association which has been a great encouragement to many Christian artists over those years.

Medieval tradition, in the various Mystery Play cycles, often gave to the shepherds' scenes a warm-hearted, comic atmosphere and this modern example is no exception. As in the Middle Ages, this comedy is not a subversion of the Incarnation, but a counterpoint to it. Not so much comic relief within a serious story, but rather expressing the truth that it is divine relief which gently invades the foolish rough-and-tumble of human existence.

This sketch is an adjunct to the events in the Bethlehem stable. It captures the turmoil into which the shepherds are thrown by the heavenly choir on the hills. They are unprepared, overwhelmed, empty-handed and, worst of all, four hours late for supper. They are well and truly caught out, not least by their waiting wives, who have calmly beaten them to it.

(LEWIN *and* SHENKYN *arrive at Lewin's home where they start rummaging through drawers, desperately searching for a gift*)

LEWIN   Look, we've got to find something. Right?

SHENKYN Can't we just go as we are, Mr Lewin?

LEWIN   As we are? Walk into the stable? The Son of God? As we are?

SHENKYN Well, like, bring ourselves!

LEWIN   Oh yes, that would be very useful. One alcoholic shepherd and one dithering idiot with an IQ of three and a half. Very useful! Just what the baby needs.

SHENKYN Well sir, Mr Lewin, if he's the Son of God, we can't really give him anything, can we?

LEWIN   Have you ever heard of the phrase, 'It's the thought that counts'?

SHENKYN Er...no.

LEWIN   No, well, I realise that thought perhaps is not your strong point, Shenkyn – but perhaps you could make an effort on this occasion. (*Spelling it out*) When we go into the presence of the Son of God, in the stable, we'll kneel, and we'll worship. Right?

SHENKYN (*Nodding slowly*) Right.

LEWIN   Right. And then we'll fumble in our pockets.

SHENKYN Right.

LEWIN   And you'll bring out a conker and two pieces of string and a snotty handkerchief.

SHENKYN Right.

LEWIN   No, WRONG. We're going to give that baby something for keeps. However small, something precious, right? *Meaningful.*

SHENKYN   (*Taking a pair of socks out of a drawer*) Are socks meaningful, Mr Lewin?

LEWIN   Only when they are stuffed in your mouth, Shenkyn.

SHENKYN   (*Dropping the socks back and pulling out a toy lamb*) What about this?

LEWIN   I made that little toy lamb myself...yessss...now that's a good idea. I think the baby would like something we've made ourselves.

SHENKYN   I could give my shepherd's staff. I carved it myself!

LEWIN   For an imbecile, you are making gigantic leaps forward, Shenkyn.

(DOREEN *and* BRENDA *arrive. A ghastly silence falls*)

DOREEN   Well?

LEWIN   (*Hastily stuffing the toy lamb into his pocket*) Well what, dear?

DOREEN   Well perhaps you'd like to elaborate on your reasons for being four hours late for supper.

LEWIN   (*Grabbing him aside*) Don't tell them where we've been, they won't understand all this angel business.

SHENKYN   (*Whispering*) But Mr Lewin, we have just seen (*getting suddenly loud*) THREE MILLION ANGE–

LEWIN	(*Hissing savagely*) It's above them, Shenkyn, that's men's stuff that is—
DOREEN	What is?
LEWIN	Nothing.
DOREEN	And where have you been doing nothing all this time?
LEWIN	Nowhere, dear.
DOREEN	Nowhere. Oh. Was it full?
LEWIN	What do you mean, my little chicken?
DOREEN	Was the nowhere you go every evening when you're late, full?
LEWIN	Oh. Oh. Oh. That! Ha, ha, ha! She's a great sense of humour my missus.
BRENDA	That's what I said when you married him, Doreen.
DOREEN	That's right, Brenda, you said I had a 'highly developed sense of humour'. So tell me how much money you spent and we can all have a laugh about it.
LEWIN	Oh no, no, my little pussycat, nothing like that, we've just, er…just been up in the hills, er, looking at the—
SHENKYN	Three million—
LEWIN	Stars, and er, meditating in the stillness.
DOREEN	That's why your face is red and you're out of breath, is it? Meditating?
LEWIN	Look, my little budgerigar, Shenkyn and I have had an 'experience'—but we can't go into it right now.

37

DOREEN	Why are you rifling through my drawers?
LEWIN	Because it's the only opportunity I get, my sunflower.
DOREEN	Very funny. We're laughing a lot at that one, aren't we Brenda.
BRENDA	Oh yes, we're so helpless we've completely forgotten that you're both four hours late for supper.
LEWIN	(*Squirming*) Well, see, it's...er, difficult to explain these deep, er, for want of a better word, *religious* matters.
DOREEN	Religious??
LEWIN	Yes.
DOREEN	You've had a *religious* experience??
LEWIN	Yes.
BRENDA	(*To* SHENKYN) *You've* had a *religious* experience???'?'?
SHENKYN	Yes, I've had one of them things as well.
BRENDA	(*To* SHENKYN) Come on then, share your 'experience'.
SHENKYN	(*Drowning*) Er...
LEWIN	(*Putting a protective arm round* SHENKYN) Ah, well, that we can't do. See? It's, well, you might not appreciate the finer points, my cherry-pie.
DOREEN	Such as?
LEWIN	Peace on earth, goodwill to *men*...men, see.
BRENDA	(*Moving uncomfortably close to* SHENKYN) So

this—mystical happening—has nothing to say to women?

SHENKYN   Er...

LEWIN   Oh yes, yes...it can be passed on...er... from the top...I mean from the men to the, er...

DOREEN   Keep going. I'm waiting for something coherent to come out.

LEWIN   (*With sudden inspiration*) EVE! That's it. Eve!

DOREEN   What?

LEWIN   Well that's where the trouble starts...see, Eve listened to the serpent, didn't she, Shenkyn?

SHENKYN   What, hissing, you mean?

LEWIN   (*Between tightly clenched teeth*) Speaking, Shenkyn.

SHENKYN   Oh. I didn't know snakes could speak.

LEWIN   They can't. This one was an exception.

SHENKYN   Oh.

BRENDA   (*To* DOREEN) My husband can always be trusted to shed light on theological questions. (*To* LEWIN) Carry on.

LEWIN   Well, there you are. Ever since Eve bungled it, women have been, er...well, couldn't be trusted with responsibility.

DOREEN   Oh yes? Well, if we're discussing responsibility, where was Adam, then?

39

BRENDA   He was probably having his eighth pint of blackberry juice with a couple of gorillas.

DOREEN   Yes, and what do you think would have happened if Adam had been around when the serpent turned up? Would he have done any better than Eve?

BRENDA   No, he would have taken three pears, two bananas and an orange as well.

DOREEN   The only difference being that he wouldn't have told Eve about it.

BRENDA   She would just have found the peel all over the floor.

LEWIN   (*Mopping himself with a handkerchief and fighting to regain control of the argument*) I think we're getting off the subject, my little nightingale, the point I'm trying—although not succeeding very well in making—is that women stay upstairs in the synagogue and men get on with the business downstairs. Now why is that?

DOREEN   That is because if women were to speak in the synagogue there is a slightly greater danger of the truth emerging.

BRENDA   They might say things like, 'No man can love God and not make his own bed'.

DOREEN   A prophet who leaves his nail clippings on the floor is a selfish little prig.

BRENDA   Things like that.

LEWIN   All right, all right, we'll tell you. If you're going to be awkward. We'll tell you the whole truth.

DOREEN	That's very generous of you.
LEWIN	We have just seen—(LEWIN *struggles for the right language*)
SHENKYN	Wait for it!...
LEWIN	We have just been privileged—personally—and deeply honoured—by the appearance to us—
SHENKYN	Me and Mr Lewin!...
LEWIN	(*The story comes flooding out suddenly*) A-private-appearance-of-three-million-angels-singing-glory-to-God-in-the-highest-hallelujah-and-peace-on-earth-good-will-to-all-men.
	(*Pause*)
DOREEN	Three million?
LEWIN	Yup.
DOREEN	Three million??
	(LEWIN *and* SHENKYN *nod with huge self-assured smiles*)
DOREEN	You're so stupid that God had to send three *million* angels to make sure you got the point?
	(*The smile goes from* MR LEWIN's *face, but not from* SHENKYN's *who doesn't get the significance of this and nods in enthusiastic agreement*)
LEWIN	Well, to be honest, my little nutkin, I hadn't seen it that way, no...no, as I see it, the angels came in such huge numbers to celebrate the birth of—

41

DOREEN	The Christ-child, yes.
LEWIN	(*Utterly amazed*) You know about this?
DOREEN	Well, don't look so shocked.
LEWIN	But—
SHENKYN	But I thought—
DOREEN	Brenda and I have known about this for weeks.
BRENDA	That's right.
LEWIN	It's impossible.
DOREEN	What's impossible? God coming into the world or women being the first to see the truth?
LEWIN	Well—I—mean…
BRENDA	Oh yes, we've been reading the scriptures. Praying. Talking together. You know. We just had a…feeling…
DOREEN	A growing certainty that the Messiah would come…
LEWIN	No angels?
DOREEN	(*As if puzzled by the question*) No.
SHENKYN	No thundering great choirs?
BRENDA	No.
LEWIN	Singing hallelujah?
DOREEN	No. Just a still small voice saying 'the time has come'.
BRENDA	And the child is here now, with us in Bethlehem.

LEWIN   (*Warily—beginning to guess their game*)
           You've had a religious experience as well!

DOREEN   Oh no, this was normal.

LEWIN   Religion? Normal??

BRENDA   We went along to see the son of God in his
           stable.

LEWIN   Whaaat??!

SHENKYN   Whaaat??!

BRENDA   We had a nice chat with Mary and Joseph.

DOREEN   It's funny really, God spoke to Mary, but
           Joseph didn't understand at first.

LEWIN   (*Panic-stricken*) Wait! Don't tell me you
           took the baby presents too!!??

BRENDA   No, we just took ourselves.

SHENKYN   That's what I said we should do, Mr
           Lewin—

LEWIN   Shut up!! And come on! At least we've got
           something over them lad!! (*Triumphantly
           taking out the toy lamb*) Yes! (*After a
           moment's reflection*) Er...yes. Come on!

SHENKYN   Shouldn't we ask them the way?

LEWIN   (*Finally losing his patience*) I KNOW THE
           WAY!!!

           (*He crashes into a doorpost and then exits
           awkwardly, followed by* SHENKYN. *Silence*)

DOREEN   You know something Brenda?

BRENDA   What's that, Doreen?

DOREEN   Well, when this story gets told...

43

BRENDA	I know what you're going to say.
DOREEN	It'll be a man that writes it.
BRENDA	Yes. And we're not going to be in it, are we?
DOREEN	No.
BRENDA	Never mind. They'll all read the unabridged version in heaven.
DOREEN	Cup of tea?
BRENDA	Thanks.

Shepherd's Delight

A YORKSHIRE SHEPHERD remembers—which is why this monologue is written as it is. Obviously this mild dialect can be transported into something that makes sense in the country or local region of your performance.

SHEPHERD It *were* a surprise, aye. We'd had a mid-dlin' sort of day, really. Usual. You know, findin' half a blade of grass and worryin' about fleas, footrot and one thing and another. The lad I work with, Daniel, had been playin' his pipe earlier.... He plays some strange tunes on that thing. I'm sure it upsets sheep. Well, by now he'd blown himself out. Sun had gone in a blaze o' glory and flock were all tucked up for t' night. I say 'flock' but it were on the com-pact side. Half a dozen. But then they get individual attention, you see, and as long as there's one to look after, I shan't be out of a job, shall I?

We were both laid down in fold door-way, so sheep couldn't get out and bears couldn't get in and one thing and another. Each man alone with his thoughts, waitin' for onset o't' night. That's my favourite time, dusk. Just slippin' quietly into night as colours drain out o' land and stars come up ever so slowly, like workin' on a piece o' silver. It's amazin' what you come out with up there on the hills. You're kind of out o't' runnin', aren't you? Well, just before it happened, there was a moment when air, like, thickened, very still and I knew there was someone there.

'Be not afraid!' he says and I jumped. Six feet. He were huge, shinin' like a cop-per kettle! He said he'd come with news about baby bein' born down in t' city. He was to be like a saviour for people and it was a great joy he said and then there were hundreds of them. All singin'. It were most peculiar. Singin' about peace on earth. Now as far as I know, we were only ones listenin'. And then they all went away. It were really very special.

So we felt we had to go and see t' bairn, because there was to be a sign, like he would be wrapped up, in a trough and that's how we found him with his father and mother but it weren't awkward, like. They were just like us and I was proud that we'd come. I mean we couldn't just of layed down again after that singin'. We said hello and told them about good news and we gave him presents. I give him a leather pouch and I suggested Daniel leave him the pipe. It were very affectin'.

On the way home, we sang. Sheep were still there. Oh, aye. I like to think that God were taking care of everyone that night.

Talking Lightly

TWO PEOPLE of any appropriate age.

Many Christians agonise about how they can subtly introduce Jesus into conversations with their friends and colleagues. Many of those friends and colleagues, of course, have no problem with this—they introduce the name of Jesus constantly into everyday life without any subtlety at all, usually as a loud curse when something goes wrong. Instead of merely wincing at this kind of thoughtless blasphemy, this sketch is an attempt to use it more constructively, as a springboard for discussion.

The sketch was originally written for two men but has worked successfully with two women, once the necessary change of names has been made. It works best if the first two words are delivered with typical venom.

(Two people are in a sitting-room. ONE is balancing on an upright chair, reaching up to change a light-bulb. TWO is sitting in an armchair with his nose in a newspaper. ONE cannot quite reach the socket so tries to stand on the back of the chair. It tips over, and everything crashes to the floor.)

ONE   Jesus Christ!

       (There is a short silence)

       You might help! *(Pause)* I said, 'You might help'.

TWO   I heard you.

ONE   Thanks for listening.

TWO   *(Still engrossed in the paper)* But since you so specifically asked someone else to give you a hand, I thought you would be okay. Especially as he claimed to be the Light of the World.

ONE   God Almighty!

TWO   *(Looking up)* That *is* the issue, isn't it? Though, of course, not everyone would give such a clear affirmation of faith. There are several other popular theories, ranging from an extra-terrestrial expression of the galactic consciousness, famous for his conjuring tricks at wedding receptions, to an astronaut, a health fanatic, an extremely good man who was particularly kind to widows and children under five, a sort of first century social worker, the founder of a weird self-sacrificing sect of mushroom-eating drug addicts, a spoke in the great wheel of Karma. Any old rubbish really.

ONE   What are you talking about?

TWO   Jesus Christ.

ONE   Whatever for?

TWO   Well, you brought him up. I was reading about Terry Venables.

ONE   Eh?

TWO   It's not entirely fair, is it? Blaming him for you being such an elephantine puddinghead as to balance your twelve and a half stone on the back of that chair. Unless it's the Creator's fault for making you five feet short of the light socket. How would you like it if I shouted your name at the top of my voice every time I made a complete doughnut of myself? 'Roger Parker!' would become synonymous with crass incompetence. Actually, that might be quite an appropriate thing to shout, really.

ONE   Charming!

TWO   Precisely. So why should he like it any more than you?

ONE   What's got into you all of a sudden? Why are you so bothered about Jesus?

TWO   I don't think you'll find that it's just me. About a third of the entire population of the world profess to follow the person who, as far as you're concerned, is merely the means to vent your frustrations over a sprained ankle.

ONE   He's dead, for Christ's sake! I mean for...Chri ...for crying out loud!

TWO   Well, no doubt you've made a careful study of the evidence for his resurrection and you're entitled to your own conclusions. On the other hand you do seem a little obsessed with the man. So come on then, what do you know about this man who's so constantly on your lips?

ONE   He was a kind of a religious leader, wasn't he?

TWO   Oh, I see. So when I spill my coffee, I could just as easily say, 'Whoops! Desmond Tutu! I've just done a Billy Graham down my trousers!'

ONE   He was a kind of revolutionary–into peace and love and fish in a big way. He wore sandals. Yeah.

TWO   Have you ever thought of publishing your research? (*Pause*) Well, perhaps you're right... I mean his active life only lasted three years, he held no position in public life, he never wrote a book, he never used force or possessed any money to speak of. He was executed.

ONE   That's right. It was on a sort of cross, wasn't it?

TWO   A sort of cross! It was the most famous death in human history. Two thousand years later the church he founded is growing faster than ever, convinced that he came back from the dead and has power to change lives and generally make the world a better place.

ONE   And you believe all that? You never told me about this before.

TWO   I'm thinking about it. What if it's true?

ONE   Oh, for God's sake!

TWO   (*Vehemently*) No! For your sake! And mine.

51

'Twoface' Malone

or

The Parable of the Unforgiving Gangster

NARRATOR
THE BOSS
MALONE
BABYFACE

Somewhere in this fast-moving little encounter is embedded the story which Jesus told of the servant who refused to forgive his friend a tiny debt, though he himself had just been released from a colossal one by the king. The contrast in the original is exaggerated for effect—almost a cartoon, a sick joke. This version of that story should be played with all the subtlety of a Sunday afternoon black and white 'B' movie. It might be embellished with whatever you think appropriate: sound effects, stripey suits, violin cases and brainless, silent minders for THE BOSS.

Jesus's story ends with judgement. The heartless servant is seized and sent to jail to reflect on his behaviour. Here the abrupt ending thrusts the responsibility for that judgement onto the audience.

(Roar of traffic, police sirens, tyres squealing)

NARRATOR   Chicago 1935. Rocky 'Twoface' Malone was a desperate man. A small matter of ten grand in phone bills, sharp suits and parking fines he owed the Boss, Hardnose Corleone.

(A door bursts open)

BOSS   Malone, you owe me ten grand. My patience has run out, Malone.

MALONE   Boss...I, er...I...ahm...this is a bad time for me, Boss.

BOSS   I'm tired of your debts, Malone. The constant whinging excuses.

MALONE   But I have the money! I mean I *had* the money, last night. It was in my pants pocket and then, whadderyerknow, my mom puts my pants in the laundry! Ten grand in white bobbly bits all over the ironing.

BOSS   I've had it with you, Malone. I can't take it any more. So I'm gonna make you an offer you can't refuse.

MALONE   No! Please, Boss, gimme more time. Please!

BOSS   Here's the offer. I'm gonna forgive you the whole debt.

MALONE   I don't wanna die! *(Pause)* Forgive me?! *Forgive* me???

BOSS   Yeah, I reckon.

MALONE   Everything?!

BOSS	The whole bang shoot.
MALONE	I can't believe I'm hearing this, Boss.
BOSS	I never go back on my word, Malone.
MALONE	I know that. I know you never go back on your word.
BOSS	It's all wiped out. There. I feel...good. I feel...yeah...like now I'll go and lie down.
MALONE	You're forgiving me the whole lot?
BOSS	Don't try my patience, Malone. Believe me.
MALONE	I mean, even those things you never got to hear about?
BOSS	What things, Malone?
MALONE	You remember those South African diamonds you asked me to deposit at the bank?
BOSS	In the green silk box with the priceless earrings?
MALONE	Yeah. The ones you said were the lost diamonds of the Zulu Warrior King.
BOSS	I remember.
MALONE	Well...I, er, lost them again. I left them unlocked in the glove box of your favourite blue cadillac.
BOSS	Why d'ya leave it unlocked?
MALONE	I stopped to pick up two chocolate chip muffins and a large coffee to go at Mac-Donald's on Main Street.

BOSS	Were you mad?
MALONE	No, I was hungry.
BOSS	You never told me this?
MALONE	Well, I never thought you'd forgive me. This is great, Boss. I never knew you had this cuddly side before!
BOSS	Malone. It appears that you are personally responsible for the recession in my organisation. I blamed a down-turn on the world markets. I sacked my staff. I shouted at my family. I tried golf. I told myself it would all come right, I could not go losing thousands of dollars for ever. And do you know, I won't go losing thousands of dollars for ever.
MALONE	(*Nervous*) But you never go back on your word, right?
BOSS	Be careful, Malone. Yeah, I forgave you. But now...I don't know how to break this to you gently, Malone. So I won't break it to you gently. I'll tell you. You're fired.
MALONE	I'm fired? You forgive me and now you tell me I'm fired?
BOSS	You're fired.
MALONE	I'm fired.
BOSS	Forgiven and fired. Get yourself a new job more suited to your talents. Maybe Mac-Donald's are taking on staff?
	(*He leaves.* MALONE *immediately shouts off-stage in the opposite direction*)
MALONE	Hey! Babyface!

BABYFACE   (*Entering*) Hi!

MALONE   Come here!

BABYFACE   How's it going, Malone?

MALONE   Not so good, Babyface. I gotta get a new job.

BABYFACE   Sounds great to me.

MALONE   So I'll need my wallet back, Babyface. The snakeskin with the Walt Disney clasp. You borrowed it. I want it now!

BABYFACE   But I don't have it on me right now, Malone.

MALONE   I want it now, Babyface!

(*He produces a machine gun*)

BABYFACE   Gimme time and I'll get it for–

(*Sudden burst of machine gunfire.* BABYFACE *falls*)

MALONE   (*Addressing the audience*) Hey, you gotta problem with this? She owed me!

Blank Cheque

PORTER, night porter of three-star hotel
WOMAN, manager of local restaurant
INJURED MAN, in his twenties

One of the most famous stories in the world, the
parable of the good Samaritan, arises quite casually it
seems out of a discussion about how to inherit eternal
life. An expert in Jewish law summarises all its intri-
cacies in the two-fold command to love God and to
love one's neighbour. Jesus commends his clear thinking as the route to eternal life. The lawyer then asks
what he believes is a more difficult question: 'Who is
my neighbour?' The story is Jesus's answer. A neighbour is anyone in need and, in particular, anyone
whom one would normally disregard or even hate. The
story is now proverbial and has been reinterpreted in
many different situations and racial conflicts.

Sometimes fresh insight can only be unlocked by
coming at a parable from an unexpected angle. This
sketch grew from the final detail of Jesus's story—the
carefree generosity of the Samaritan, effectively handing the innkeeper a 'blank cheque' to provide for the
injured man's welfare. Although it doesn't concentrate
on the central issue of the parable, the sketch clearly
implies that the woman, who is here the Samaritan,
has had to cross several cultural barriers in order to
fulfil the command to love her neighbour.

(*A* WOMAN *assists a badly injured* MAN *into a chair in the hotel foyer. The injured* MAN *is poorly dressed and barely conscious. A* PORTER *is asleep behind the reception desk. Having attempted to stanch a head wound with her handkerchief, the* WOMAN *leaves the* MAN *seated stage left and approaches the desk. She rings the bell and wakes the snoring* PORTER)

PORTER   (*Getting up suddenly*) Can I help you, sir? Er, I mean, can I help you madam?

WOMAN   A single room, please.

PORTER   (*Yawns*) Tonight?

WOMAN   I know it's late.

PORTER   Just for one night is it, madam?

WOMAN   I don't know yet. It might be several.

PORTER   (*Notices the man*) Excuse me a moment. Oi! Now you get out of it! What do you take this place for!

(WOMAN *tries to get between* PORTER *and* MAN)

WOMAN   He's the one who needs the room.

PORTER   I'm sorry, madam, we don't want trouble here. (*To the* MAN) Now listen, friend—

WOMAN   (*Desperately searching for her cheque book*) How much is it?

PORTER   More than my job's worth.

WOMAN   I'm just paying for the room!

PORTER   Full board is £69.

WOMAN   I think that should cover it, then.

(*She hands* PORTER *cheque*)

PORTER   This is blank!

WOMAN   You fill it in when he leaves. There's my address.

(MAN *groans*)

PORTER   No, I'm sorry, we can't have this.

(PORTER *moves to eject* MAN. WOMAN *bars the way*)

WOMAN   Give him whatever he needs for as long as he wants.

PORTER   Is he a relative?

WOMAN   I found him lying in the street outside. I was on my way home from work.

PORTER   Oh, yes. (*He smirks. There is a pause. He turns abruptly and fetches key from behind desk, banging it down*) Room 209 then.

WOMAN   Let's get him into the lift, shall we?

PORTER   I shouldn't be doing this.

(*They help the injured* MAN *to his feet*)

Did you bring him here on your own?

WOMAN   A few people walked past, but I think the blood rather put them off. I'll phone for a doctor.

PORTER   (*Steps back, wiping his hands*) You sure you shouldn't be phoning the police?

WOMAN   I think that would make things worse at the moment, don't you?

PORTER   This isn't anything to do with drugs, is it?

WOMAN   Judging by the state of his arm, I think that might be a fair assumption, yes.

PORTER Filth.

WOMAN   Look, if you'd rather not help…

PORTER I'd rather not catch anything, if you don't mind.

        (*The* MAN *collapses again into the chair. The* WOMAN *tries to keep the handkerchief to his head*)

WOMAN   Perhaps you'd like to phone the doctor, then.

        (PORTER *watches her, still wiping his hands*)

        Well, go on.

PORTER Have you got kids?

WOMAN   Yes, two. Why?

PORTER Well, violence, drugs, Aids…Not the nicest kind of world for their mother to be involved in, is it? You ought to be setting them a good example.

        (WOMAN *stops tending the wound and looks hard at the* PORTER. *Silence*)

        I'll phone the doctor.

        (*He picks up the phone*)

        (*All freeze*)

The Burning Fiery Furnace

The style of this narrative lyric may give inspiration for similar treatments of other stories. It could be performed to a simple rhythmic accompaniment, to your own musical setting or to the original one by Chris Norton. This was in a musical which Riding Lights presented to Pathfinder groups, entitled *The Grand Slam*. (This music is available from the same PO Box address given on the page about obtaining a performing licence at the front of this book.) Whatever you do with it, however many quivering drumkits and relentless body-poppers are involved, keep it 'up front', jokey, fast and brash.

There was a king who somewhat lost his grip
And made a serious doctrinal slip
A huge image of himself for worship
To be honest, a downright ego trip.

> *Beat that!*
> *Wot a crazy story!*
> *But you better believe it 'cos it's true*
> *And the message of it applies to you.*

I am God, he said, everyone keep calm
Worship me, there's no need for alarm
A nutcase with a certain kind of charm
In fact, he didn't mean a lot of harm.

Now if any person did not comply
Nebuchadnezzar said they'd have to fry
For he had got an oven switched up high
'So worship me', he said, 'and don't be shy'.

> *Beat that!* Etc.

Shadrach, Meshach and Abednego
Weren't the sort of lads to stoop so low.
They were worshippers of God and so
Due to their commitments couldn't go.

But Nebby was a pyromaniac
And every now and then he'd get a bad attack
So when he saw them pray behind his back
He thought he'd light the fuse and stand well back.

> *Beat that!* Etc.

Our heroes didn't get themselves uptight
'Even if we do have to fry tonight',
They simply said, 'We've done what's right.'
The king replied, 'Er, have you got a light?'

Our friends came home to a real fire
A warm reception as the flames grew higher
Frankly, their situation was rather dire
It looked like time for the heavenly choir.

Nebuchadnezzar rubbed his hands with glee
This was better than Neighbours on TV
But then he got another show for free
There were four in the fire instead of three!

Beat that! Etc.

Our plucky little worshippers of God
Did not find this guest appearance odd
They knew He wouldn't leave them on their tod
And so He sent along this other bod.

Beat that! Etc.

See with this angel geyser in the heat
It damped the roaring furnace down a treat
Instead of roasting like a joint of meat
They were cool as cucumbers, which was neat.

Now all this showed up Nebby as a fraud
His party had been gate-crashed by the Lord
Flaming miracles cannot be ignored
And so he had to grudgingly applaud.

Beat that!
Wot a crazy story!
But you'd better believe it 'cos it's true
And the message of it applies to you!

The Great
Commission
(Parts 205, 206)

JACK, an unsuspecting neighbour
MR DAI EVANS, master of the conversation-stopper.

The following two sketches are illustrations from a much larger book (which we have not yet come across): *Five Hundred Excellent Ways to Hinder the Great Commission of Jesus.*

(MR EVANS *is working in his garden. His next door neighbour approaches him cheerfully. Sunshine. Birdsong. The joys of spring*)

JACK   Morning, Mr Evans.

MR EVANS   (*With deep seriousness*) Hullo, Jack.

JACK   Doing a bit of digging, then?

MR EVANS   That's right.

JACK   Grand day for it. Digging. The smell in the air. The dew still on the grass. Makes you feel good to be alive, doesn't it?

            (JACK *inhales the spring freshness with satisfaction.* MR EVANS *stops working and looks at* JACK *intently*)

MR EVANS   No. I'm afraid not, Jack. Feelings are immaterial. What matters is whether each one of us is right with God.

JACK   I beg your pardon?

MR EVANS   (*Awesomely doom-laden*) You might well but you would be wrong. It's God's pardon you should be begging. We may all *feel* good now and then, but the truth is that none of us is good, (*his voice quivers with emotion*) for the Bible says that, 'All have sinned and fallen short of the glory of God', Romans three, twenty-three. Have you read Romans, Jack?

JACK   Er...no, I've not read any of his. Good are they?

MR EVANS   Jack. I'm glad that we can talk like this, out in the open.

65

JACK	(*Casting a bemused glance around the garden*) Oh, aye.
MR EVANS	I know that humanly speaking it's a lovely day. The birds are singing and all seems right with the world. But let me ask you bluntly, are you happy, Jack?
JACK	Well, yes...I...er...
MR EVANS	(*With a remorseless look, that would pierce* JACK's *very soul*) I mean *really happy*—deep down inside!
JACK	(*Nervously*) I've had a bit of trouble with me gallstones, recently, but nothing to... er...
MR EVANS	I'm talking about *spiritual* gallstones, Jack.
JACK	Ooh, no, I've not had any of them.
MR EVANS	Do you see that rotten apple lying over there, Jack? To me, that apple is just a tiny illustration of the condition of the human heart.
JACK	(*Innocently*) Is it Granny Smith's?
MR EVANS	Possibly. But it could also be Jack Sowerby's! (*Hoarsely*) I feel that God is trying to speak to you through that rotten apple, Jack.
JACK	(*Without the faintest idea of what he is talking about*) Well, ha ha. He'll have to speak up a bit, then!
MR EVANS	I'm serious, Jack. God can see the maggot in your life.

(*A meaningful pause*)

Now imagine for a moment that, instead of digging my turnips this morning, I am digging your grave!!

(JACK *swallows*)

It's a sobering thought, isn't it? You see, the sunshine makes you feel good to be alive, but how will you feel when you are dead?

JACK   Not so good, I suppose.

MR EVANS   The Bible says that you are already dead. That you are, shall we say, already 'Jack-in-the-box'.

(*There is a brief shared moment of anxious laughter*)

JACK   (*Through the hysteria*) Oh, that's very good...

MR EVANS   (*Suddenly serious*) That's not so funny either, Jack. Because, like those flowers along the path, one day we shall all be picked. The question is, which vase will *you* be put in. Think about it.

(JACK *edges offstage as* MR EVANS *continues to glare after him before continuing his digging*)

67

TIM, a hopeful teenager
MIKE, a youth leader with vision for 'personal work'.

(*A young teenager approaches his youth group leader. The leader is somewhat earnest and fresh-faced. His obtrusive new trainers betray a deep desire to win the confidence of fourteen-year-olds*)

TIM   Hey, Mike, can I ask you something?

MIKE   Sure. (*Needlessly assuming a jokey American accent*) Go right ahead, kid!

TIM   I've been thinking...

MIKE   Get away! (*Realising that humour is not creating quite the right response*) No, sorry. Go on.

TIM   You know what you were saying last week about Jesus living inside us?

MIKE   Yup.

TIM   Well, I'd like that to happen to me.

MIKE   Yup.

TIM   Yeah.

MIKE   Really? (*He is genuinely flustered by such an unexpected and direct interest in something other than table-tennis*) Are you sure? I mean, great! That's...that's...great! Um...

TIM   I don't understand. Is he inside me already?

MIKE   Er...no. No, he's not. Not unless you've asked him in already. No.

TIM   Well, I'd like to.

MIKE   Good.

       (*Pause*)

TIM Yeah.

MIKE (*His mind awash with fragments of his Bible College Evangelism course*) That's great. But you need to be absolutely sure that you know what you're doing, Tim, before you do it. I mean, you understand about the Cross, don't you, Tim? And the whole Jewish sacrificial system and how the High Priest laid his hands on the scapegoat, so that when Isaiah says, 'God laid on him...' er, not the goat in this case, but Jesus...'the iniquity of us all', that is how forgiveness can work...in our lives...Tim. That's all clear to you, is it?

TIM (*Quietly confident*) Yeah.

MIKE Great. So...um...

TIM So, why are you sweating?

MIKE Now look, Tim. Let's get this straightened out and on the table. Becoming a Christian is very simple. That's the wonderful thing about it, really. It's so simple that even a fool could become a Christian, Tim. And many do. It's just the three points: A, B, C, D. Let's take a cool look at them one by one, shall we? Firstly—

TIM A.

MIKE Exactly. A. Admit. (*With real seriousness*) You need to admit, Tim, that you are a sinner.

TIM I know.

MIKE (*Slightly thrown*) Good. Well, that's the first point, then. Secondly, B. Believe. You must believe in...er...in God, obviously and in Jesus and in the...er...sacrificial business we've just talked about and in the removal of

69

sin and guilt from each of us in the Holy Spirit, which art in heaven, hallowed be thy name.

TIM What's C for?

MIKE Yes, I'm coming to that. Well, of course, C is for...is for, um...we have to *see* ourselves, you see, as needing God's forgiveness. And so finally F. I'm sorry, D. Now D is very interesting. D stands for Dedicate.

TIM What's that mean?

MIKE Precisely. So let me draw a diagram for you here. Have you got a piece of paper and a pencil? No. Well, never mind. (*With sudden inspiration*) Tim. I want you to imagine that this mug of orange squash represents my sin. Now I shall need a little bit of room to demonstrate this, but repentance means turning *right round* (*As he gives dramatic force to his theology, the drink slips out of his hand*) Ah. My sin is now all over the carpet. Um. Don't worry about that, Tim, let's just pray together, shall we? Be careful where you kneel though. It's a bit wet.

(*They kneel in prayer. Freeze*)

The King's Banquet

MAID
WAITRESS
STEWARD
BUTLER
DANCERS
CHEF
FLORENCE
SERVANTS

Much is made of parties in the Bible. Feasts, banquets, meals and weddings are not only occasions for human celebration, they are also often symbols for heaven itself and the hope of eternal joy in the presence of God. This is one of two sketches in this book based on the memorable parable Jesus told of the magnificent banquet, lovingly prepared, to which all the invited guests refused to come. However, in this version there is a major twist, for which we crave artistic licence: the invitations were never delivered.

Instead of the privileged guests, through their own ingratitude, failing to respond to the King's invitation, here it is the King's own servants who let him down. They are so preoccupied with the details of preparing the banquet, that they fail to spread the word. This may ring bells with those who have experienced missions and other evangelistic activities where the organisation is frenetic, thousands of pounds are

71

spent, and yet publicity materials sit around in depressing heaps long after they should have been distributed; the event largely attended by those who would have come anyway. Telling others about the banquet should be the easy part. So often this is the last thing we think of.

(Preparations are being made for a splendid banquet. People rush in and out with trays, bottles, streamers and balloons. Much commotion. In the middle of all this activity, the head WAITRESS *and* STEWARD *are checking through the menu for the last time.)*

MAID   *(Passing with pile of tablecloths, to audience)* The Kingdom of Heaven is like a king who gave a great banquet and invited many. *(She leaves)*

WAITRESS   Fifteen roast duck.

STEWARD   Duck. Roast. Fifteen!

WAITRESS   Three huntsman pies and pickles

STEWARD   Pies, huntsman. Three. Pickle and!

WAITRESS   Two grilled sheep.

STEWARD   Sheep grilled. One pair!

WAITRESS   Stuffed pheasant Mozambique *avec apricot sauce cardinale.*

STEWARD   Er, yup. Some of that.

WAITRESS   Two fried chicken and water chestnuts.

STEWARD   Number eighty-six. Twice!

WAITRESS   Roast ox in chocolate mousse.

STEWARD   One beef in brown!

BUTLER   *(Rushing on in quite a state)* Is the King's Courier there? Excuse me, is the King's Courier...What are you standing around here for?

STEWARD   Just checking the menu.

BUTLER   Well, there's no time for that now. Go and

73

make sure the wine is chilled. (*To* WAIT-RESS) The melons have all got pips in! Do I have to do everything myself? (*To* STEW-ARD) Yes, today! And nothing but the best, do you hear? Prime vintage. Quickly. (*Exit* STEWARD) Look, is the King's Courier here? (*Consulting large list*) Dancers, ho! Minstrels, ho! Oh, never mind. The King's Courier? Have you seen the...look! I'm trying to organise a banquet. The whole thing is chaotic! Chaotic! I'm looking for the King's Courier. Are you the King's Courier?

DANCER   No dear, I'm the King's Couriographer.

BUTLER   Oh, for goodness sake! Well, you'll just have to go and couriograph somewhere else. I've got the flower people in here in a minute.

DANCER   But we haven't rehearsed the final dance. My *pas de deux*!

BUTLER   I'm terribly sorry, but we're far too busy. Just go away. This is frantic!

WAITRESS (*Returning*) He's got mumps.

BUTLER   Who has?

WAITRESS The King's Courier.

BUTLER   Oh, for crying out loud, how on earth are we going to tell all the guests that we're ready for them? Well, *you'll* have to be the Kung's Cirrier, I mean King's Curryer. Oh, for heaven's sake, just go and summon all the bests to the Gang's Kinquet!! Oh, ptherrr!! There's only another two

74

	hours to go and nobody's RSVP'd yet. So cut along.
WAITRESS	You mean, 'come for all is now ready!'?
BUTLER	Yes, that's the sort of thing.

(*Exit* WAITRESS *almost bumping into a French* CHEF *advancing on the* BUTLER *with a carving knife.* FLORENCE, *his assistant, carries a huge soup tureen*)

Now who are you? Are you the flower people?

CHEF	What do you min am I ze Fleur peopul? Stupid Butlerr! I am wanting to know who is putting sree sousand begonias on my cheesbore. Ze kitchen look like les jardins botaniques! You and your stupid fleur peopul! Take them, or I tell Florence to pur mershrerm zerp over ze carpette! Oui, Florence?
FLORENCE	Oui, we tip it.
CHEF	Huh?
FLORENCE	Huh.
CHEF	Huh!

(*Exeunt*)

| BUTLER | Huhh...yes, dead loss these foreigners. (*Shouting off*) Get the begonias shifted, would you? Somebody's put them all over his cheesebore. (*To audience*) Most odd that nobody's RSVP'd yet. I mean we're laying on a decent spread here...twenty roast hogs, *avocado soufflé Hollandais*, what's the matter with everybody? It's |

absolutely wizard. Still, I'm sure they'll all be here come eight o'clock. EIGHT O'CLOCK!! Good heavens! I've got five thousand *chaises longues* to shift before then and all those laughing bears to feed. Don't laugh if you don't feed them, laughing bears. They go all grizzly, aha ha ha h-oh. That's how you get grizzly bears, you see, aha ha h- well, please yourselves. Must have had some replies by now. The King will be here in an hour to receive the guests.

(*The* WAITRESS *returns, out of breath*)

Are you back already?

WAITRESS	Yes, erm…it's about the guests…er…
BUTLER	I thought you were supposed to be summoning them all.
WAITRESS	I have. I knocked on lots of doors and I rang the big bell in the market place.
BUTLER	Thank goodness for that. At least somebody's actually lending a hand. This whole thing is becoming a nightmare.
WAITRESS	I shouldn't worry. There's nothing you can do now. Just relax.
BUTLER	Relax! This is taking ten years off my life, I can feel it.
WAITRESS	Nobody's coming.
BUTLER	And they'll probably want special cocktails, special vegetarian dishes and personalised cloakroom tickets. You just wait. What did you say?

WAITRESS	Nobody's coming.
BUTLER	Not coming?
WAITRESS	No.
BUTLER	Who's not coming?
WAITRESS	All of them.
BUTLER	All of them not coming?
WAITRESS	Is this a quiz?
BUTLER	I warn you, I am on a very short fuse. It is nearly eight o'clock and this is no time for assing about. If you are saying to me that all the guests are not coming to the King's banquet, then I shall have something very serious to say about the matter.
WAITRESS	That's what I'm saying.
BUTLER	Then I am speechless. Those people are the most unutterable, ungrateful, rude, ignorant, pathetic, despicable bounders in the history of professional catering! What will the King say? It's outrageous! (*Ripping up menu*) Stuffed pheasant Mozambique! Hollandaise sauce! They'd better come up with some mighty fine excuses, that's all I can say! Or they'll find themselves very highly strung indeed.
WAITRESS	They've only got one.
BUTLER	Hmmn?
WAITRESS	Nobody had an invitation.
BUTLER	Nonsense. The King commissioned all his servants to deliver those invitations personally, in my hearing, weeks ago!

(*Sarcastically*) Never received an invitation. We'll soon see about that. SERVANTS!!

(*Enter* SERVANTS 1 *and* 2)

Thank you. Now I am told that despite the likelihood of multiple cardiac arrests preparing for this little soirée, this is of no consequence since nobody is actually coming. On account of the fact that nobody claims to know the first thing about it. However, this is complete hogwash because I know that you delivered all those invitations weeks ago, as requested by His Majesty. Correct?

MAID   (*To audience*) And they all alike began to make excuse.

(*Awkward pause filled by coughing and shuffling from* SERVANTS)

SERVANT 1   Well, we were very much behind the idea...weren't we?

SERVANT 2   Yes, certainly.

SERVANT 1   An excellent idea...to...

WAITRESS   (*Helpfully*) Invite people to the banquet.

SERVANT 2   But, you see, I was personally far too busy getting everything ready to have time to...

WAITRESS   Deliver any...

SERVANT 1   Precisely. We prayed about it, of course, but, er...

SERVANT 2   Didn't know anybody to invite when it came to it.

SERVANT 1	Can't go dragging people in off the streets to a King's banquet, can you?
SERVANT 2	Couldn't see ourselves getting involved in that sort of thing.
SERVANT 1	Too heavily committed elsewhere.
BUTLER	I see.
SERVANT 1	I rather hoped that someone else was doing the inviting.
BUTLER	And the invitations you were supposed to give out??
SERVANT 1	I've got a few here actually, if anybody's interested?
	(*Silence*)
SERVANT 2	Well, I hope that somebody does turn up. It seems such a shame…
SERVANT 1	To waste all this…
SERVANT 2	The King must feel awful…
BUTLER	Get out! Get out!
	(*They freeze*)
MAID	How are they to hear without a preacher? And how are they to believe in him of whom they have never heard?

79

Knock-Knock:
Who Cares?
by Nigel Forde

THE MASTER
CANDLECOMBE, his senior steward,

CRABWOOD
MRS CLYSTER
ALICE   } GUESTS
QUENTIN
GALADRIEL

In contrast to the previous sketch, this is a more orthodox treatment of the parable in Luke's Gospel of the Great Banquet. Together they begin to illustrate the various ways in which the same source material can be reworked dramatically for a different audience. In this case, the challenge is directed at a society which is too self-centred, too obdurate, too busy, too small-minded to respond to the love of God. For those who find it hard to imagine what heaven might be like, part of the joy of this sketch is that it begins to colour in the details; part of the melancholy is in considering each specially prepared 'place' in heaven which might be unappreciated and empty.

Ingenuity will be required of the director to devise a stylised means of coping with all the various exits and entrances without resorting to something that looks like a changing-room.

(THE MASTER *and* CANDLECOMBE *enter separately*)

THE MASTER   That's it! Done! Finished!

CANDLECOMBE   Concluded, accomplished, fulfilled, complete...

THE MASTER   Thank you, Candlecombe; no need to paint the lily.

CANDLECOMBE   'Paint the lily'! I've never heard that quoted correctly before.

THE MASTER   Accuracy, Candlecombe. It's my watchword. Precision in all things.

CANDLECOMBE   No detail too insignificant.

THE MASTER   No avenue too dark to explore.

CANDLECOMBE   No stone too small to remain unturned.

THE MASTER   Exactly. And never more true than now.

                (*Flings papers down in front of* CANDLECOMBE)

CANDLECOMBE   Sir?

THE MASTER   The Banquet, Candlecombe!

CANDLECOMBE   Tonight?

THE MASTER   And every last detail in place. What a banquet it will be! The fruit of a lifetime's planning and preparation.

CANDLECOMBE   (*Rifling through the arrangements*) It's magnificent—wonderful. But then you've always been generous, sir, if I may say so. Presents at Christmas, Easter, Harvest; reminders of your

	affection. And the things you've done for them that they never even realised.
THE MASTER	Yes, yes, but nothing will surpass this. I've known them all so long, you see; all their desires, all their delights are as familiar to me as my own. And tonight they will discover them again. Every individual has been catered for.
CANDLECOMBE	So I see. Stuffed guinea-fowl for some; eggs, chips and mushy peas for those who prefer it.
THE MASTER	Oh, the food is easy. But look. A steam railway for Ellie, Donald and Richard; water meadows for Sally Gates and Mrs Pritchett; a jazz-band for Leo and Madge; complete silence for Mrs Doughty. And old Mr Enever: he heard a nightingale once–only once–when he was courting Mary Lawford. He's never forgotten it. Tonight he'll hear it again with Mary beside him. What was the sweetest moment of Alice Delderfield's life?
CANDLECOMBE	Well...I couldn't really tell you.
THE MASTER	And nor could Alice if you asked her. But I remember. A tiny thing. One summer, after a terrible grief, she took a drink from a mountain spring. Perfection. Tonight she will drink again. Look at the lists: no one has been forgotten. Even as we speak the bagpipe band is arriving.
CANDLECOMBE	The bagpipe band...?

THE MASTER	For old Mrs McRae. Execrable taste you may say, but if a bagpipe band warms the heart of Mrs McRae, then she shall have it. Now, off you go with the guest-list.
CANDLECOMBE	Isn't it just a *bit* late to be sending out invitations?
THE MASTER	Oh the invitations went out months ago. I want to tell them how much we are looking forward to their company. I've had the fun of planning it—you pick them up, enjoy their anticipation. Off you go.
	(THE MASTER *leaves.* CANDLECOMBE *turns to knock at the first door*)
CRABWOOD	Oh, it's you. I've had yer fancy invitation and I'll tell you what I think of it. I think it's an unwarranted and pompous piece of intrusion.
CANDLECOMBE	Ah.
CRABWOOD	I mean, who does he think he is, eh? Playing the feudal lord. Mr Bountiful sending out gracious invitations. We live in a democracy now you know—I don't have to kow-tow to anybody. I don't want to see him and you can tell him to mind his own business and let me get on with mine.
	(*Slams the door shut*)
CANDLECOMBE	Mmmmm. Probably a 'no' for that one.
	(*Knocks at another door*)

CANDLECOMBE	Mrs Clyster? I've come about the Banquet tonight.
MRS CLYSTER	Oh yes. I must say it seems a quite extraordinary idea.
CANDLECOMBE	Sorry?
MRS CLYSTER	That he should think that we're the sort of people who'd fit in at a place like that. We'd be a laughing stock. I've seen the sort of people he attracts to his functions. Frankly I'd rather die than be seen there.
	(*Exit*)
CANDLECOMBE	Not an unattractive idea. Ah—now...
	(*Knocks at another door*)
ALICE	Yes? Who is it?
CANDLECOMBE	Is that Alice Delderfield?
ALICE	(*Speaking nervously through a chained door*) Yes. My husband's not in.
CANDLECOMBE	It's about the invitation for tonight.
ALICE	Oh, yes...it sounds lovely.
CANDLECOMBE	The car's here if you're ready.
ALICE	Ohh...it's Jack you see. We'd be out of place, he says. It's kind of you, but it's not really for us, is it?
CANDLECOMBE	It's for both of you; but you can come without Jack. It's going to be wonderful.
ALICE	Oh, I can imagine. But it would upset...things. You know. I hope you

have a really nice time. At one time I'd...well, anyway...

(Shuts door quietly)

CANDLECOMBE   Not a single one in four hours. *(Noticing a passer by)* Oh, excuse me sir...? Did you get an invitation to the Banquet?

QUENTIN   Oh, yah. Nice guy. Really nice guy. Got a lot of time for him.

CANDLECOMBE   Mainly in 1999.

QUENTIN   Yah, well, the diary is a bit chocker. Got a window next week. Could we do lunch on Thursday? No? Ok, well, keep in touch, eh? Give me a bell sometime. Cheers.

CANDLECOMBE   One more.

(Knocks.)

GALADRIEL   Oh, I know what you've come for. Parties! Banquets! Is that all you can think about? Talk about fiddling while Rome burns. Some of us happen to think there are more important things to do in today's socio-economic climate. Here—you can have your invite back. And re-cycle it!

(Slams the door in his face)

CANDLECOMBE   *(Shouting in the street)* Listen! All of you, listen! I don't know what you are all expecting from this banquet but whatever it is, I promise you it will be beyond your wildest imaginings. It's...it's not just *for* you, it's *about*

86

you. You're all so busy being socially acceptable and correct and successful and bored out of your minds, you've never stopped to ask yourselves what will make you really happy, what it is you want to find. This banquet is for you, whatever you've lost, whatever you long for. This banquet is home. It's crystal glasses and white table-cloths, but it's a picnic hamper in the meadow as well. For you it's a lake and a mountain, for you it's a fireside, for you it's the winter constellations and a child in your arms. As for me— I've done. You've been offered your heart's desire, but if you want what you've already got then keep it. And don't ever ask what you might have had.

(*We hear murmurs as the crowd disperses.* CANDLECOMBE *sinks to his knees. Behind him* THE MASTER *has re-entered*)

CANDLECOMBE ...And then we all went back to where we came from—and there you have it.

THE MASTER Not one acceptance.

CANDLECOMBE Nearly one: but in the end, no. Fear, indifference, ingratitude.

THE MASTER Then the rewards shall go elsewhere.

CANDLECOMBE I'm not sure...

THE MASTER The banquet is about to begin. Bring in the guests.

CANDLECOMBE	Sir?
THE MASTER	Didn't you see a figure or two huddled in a shop doorway? No women on the street corners? Not a drunk or a beggar? No orphans, refugees? Bring them in, Candlecombe. Fill my house and my gardens with tears and I will turn them to laughter. You didn't force before; now tell everybody – use all your powers of persuasion. Shout it, whisper it! There is still time.

(We hear the sound of a nightingale)

Listen! There! The nightingale that Mr Enever heard when he courted Mary Lawford.

CANDLECOMBE	Beautiful.
THE MASTER	Oh yes. But empty. What's it worth without the delight of Mr Enever?

Prayer Link

JENNIFER, a young woman working in a missionary hospital

MEMBERS OF PRAYER MEETING, this can be a sizeable group but must include:

MAURICE

LYNN

STEVE

It is tempting to wonder what many missionaries, working far from home, would feel if they attended the meetings that occasionally gather to pray for them. Some might be grateful that anyone is praying at all. Others would despair at the perfunctory, unimaginative nature of much that goes on. This sketch is intended to stir up dead prayer meetings. It will benefit from being played with as much realism and as little caricature as possible.

(The stage is divided into two areas. On one side, JENNIFER, *a missionary in a hospital, is sitting writing a letter. On the other side, members of her church at home are meeting to pray for her)*

JENNIFER   *(Reading over what she has just written)* 'It's really hot and sticky now. The monsoon rains should break in a few weeks time, but meanwhile we enjoy the occasional evening tropical storm which cools things down. This is a demanding time of year in Pohtundra—just living is tiring and there are lots of cases of diarrhoea and other minor diseases around…*(writing)*…which sap our meagre resources of energy…'

MEETING   *(Singing the final verse of well-known hymn)*
Revive Thy work, O Lord.
Give Pentecostal showers.
The glory shall be all Thine own,
The blessing, Lord, be ours!

JENNIFER   'The new Maternity Unit is still subject to the whims of government bureaucracy and the pressure on existing facilities increases daily as refugees stream in from the north. The condition of some of them is heartbreaking. There's so little we can do…'

MAURICE   Welcome to our meeting. As you may know, we've just received word from our sister Jennifer Mayhew out in…in…um…from abroad. Unfortunately, I forgot to bring it with me. But there are certainly still a few problems at the hospital since we last prayed, so we'll have to redouble our efforts.

LYNN   I've got a copy of her letter here, if it's any
            help?

MAURICE   Oh, that's marvellous, thank you.

LYNN   The situation sounds quite serious, actually.
            Hunger and disease among the refugees...
            er...(*reading*)...'The condition of some of
            them is heartbreaking. There's so little we
            can do...'

JENNIFER   (*Continuing seamlessly*)...with the medical
            help available to us from overseas. Some
            of the other missionaries actually working
            in the camps say they can do little more
            than comfort the dying by trying to...

LYNN   ...'show them the tender love of Christ.'

STEVE   Praise God!

MAURICE   Amen. Well, let's join together and pray
            for the work over there in...in...um...in
            this part of the world. (*He stands to pray*)
            Father God, we thank and praise you that
            we can bring our sister Jennifer before
            your throne, praising you that you have
            called her out of our fellowship to serve
            you in...in...um...across the seas. May
            she be a mighty light for your gospel–(*His
            prayer fades under*)

JENNIFER   'My thoughts are obviously with you all a
            lot at this time of year. Evenings in my
            room are often quite lonely, but any letter
            is a great encouragement. Even a few
            lines.'

MAURICE   ...May she know your constant guiding
            hand upon her day by day. And may all
            the people of...this dark land come to

	know you through her work. Through Jesus Christ Our Lord. Amen.
TOGETHER	Amen.
JENNIFER	'Sometimes it's hard not to feel bitter about the very slow progress we are making in the villages around Pohtundra. To preach the gospel openly is, of course, forbidden by law...'
STEVE	Lord we pray that you will also give her time to relax. To withdraw from the daily pressures – perhaps in the evenings, Lord, to be refreshed by your presence...
JENNIFER	'...and many of the women are afraid to bring their babies to the hospital. Last week, I made the two-day journey up to the mountain village of Hindirakesh, where you may remember I asked you to pray for Kumi, the only Christian lady there. I discovered that she had died a few weeks before and so there was no one to persuade the others to trust me. On the way home I cried.'
STEVE	I forget her name, Lord, but that doesn't matter because she is known to you, so we also remember that old Christian lady in the mountains, on whom so much –
LYNN	(*Whispers into his ear*)
STEVE	I see. Father God, we are saddened by this news and we pray that you will raise up many more to stand in her place. Amen.
	(*Pause*)

MAURICE   Lord, we pray for all missionaries, every-
           where, whatever their needs. Amen.

           (*Pause*)

LYNN   Dear God, please bless all those people
           who are frightened to become Christians
           because of what may happen to them.
           Thinking especially of Muhaliya and his
           family.

MAURICE   Amen. (*Abruptly concluding the prayer
           time*) Well, thanks very much for coming
           along. See you all in due course. Good-
           night, Lynn. Well done with the letter!

           (*They all leave*)

JENNIFER   'Please continue to pray for us. God's
           work is slow but sure here. My love to you
           all, Jennifer.' (*She finishes the letter, folds it
           up and then prays, her eyes still open*) Thank
           you for being with me today. Thank you
           for helping me to stay awake long enough
           to finish the letter. You know I'm worried
           about Muhaliya having the Bible. Please
           give me the courage to let him have it
           when I see him tomorrow. I'm sorry that
           sometimes I don't feel like serving you
           very much. Help me to stop trying to work
           in my own strength. (*She puts the letter in
           an envelope and seals it up*) Amen.

The Announcement

MR POULTON, a lay leader in any local congregation

Mr Poulton's self-appointed mission is to ensure the smooth running of his local church while it waits for the appointment of a new minister. Here he deals with 'the notices'. Throughout his speech, although we never hear any of the brief interruptions, he is constantly receiving corrections and advice from different parts of the audience, usually from the back. Sometimes he pauses for information; occasionally he seems rattled but ploughs on, covering an increasing air of resignation with increasingly wooden smiles. Sometimes the changes of tack, forced upon him 'from the floor', barely interrupt the flow of his sentence; with one challenger (Betty Simpson), his flow breaks down altogether. Throughout he remains crisp and warm, though the beads of sweat appearing on his temples denote some internal stress.

(He takes up a prominent position at the front and beams reassuringly.)

MR POULTON   I don't want to take up any more time but there is one final notice which I must make absolutely clear, to avoid any confusion. *(He clears his throat)* Excuse me. Now, as you already know, the old Missionary Midweek Prayer Meeting has now become what is to be known as the E and O Group. This, I am reliably informed, stands for the Evangelism and Outreach Group. *(He cups an ear)* I'm sorry? 'Focus'?? Is it? Oh. Thank you. *(He returns his attention to the congregation)* Well, I stand corrected. This is apparently not the E and O Group at all but is the Evangelism and Outreach *Focus*.

Now we intend that this should be a regular meeting, sorry, 'focus'...is that really right, Betty? It is focus. Right. *(He nods)* Now we intend to hold these, erm, *(Making sure he's got the correct plural)* focusseses on the third Wednesday of every month at eight o'clock in the church lounge. Sorry, eight fifteen. I beg your pardon? Seven forty-five? So, it's not eight fifteen, it's a quarter *to*? Well, look, which is it—quarter to, quarter past?...You're sure about that? So it's seven forty-five p.m. on Wednesday in—oh, by the way, I should in fact say that this first week is different, because of the Pathfinders, who will be in the church lounge on the third Wednesday. But normally they will switch to the second Wednesday, leaving the church lounge free. Sorry? Church vestry, thank you. This is to avoid any confusion over our first focus.

So make a note, then, this week we will be gathering in the vestry.... At Betty Simpson's?? (*Addressing one individual sharply*) Why on earth are we going there? Oh, I see, yes. Yes. Fine. Right-o. Yes. Yes. No. (*Back to the larger group*) Apparently, Betty says she is unable to provide a cup of coffee for us in the vestry and as a further incentive I understand that she is also hoping to furnish our first focus with some delicious cakes left over from the Autumn Sale of Work.... Scones. I'm sorry. Delicious scones. So we warmly invite you all then for coffee and scones, to be followed by a time of prayer and biscuits. I mean focus. Prayer and focus.

So let's be quite clear about this, then. It's seven forty-five p.m. this Wednesday, but not the next one, at Betty Simpson's, otherwise we will be in the church lounge. (*He smiles*) Last week, we were delighted to hear from Lynda Francis and Barry Catterill who are currently serving overseas in Shanghai and Glasgow.... Sorry? Hong Kong. Sorry, Shanghai and Hong Kong. Could I also say that copies of Jeremy and Margaret Hanson's recent letter... will *not* be available...but *can be obtained* subsequently from Donald and Naomi Wentworth. Willetts. That's it.

The Willetts. Anything else, then, before I go? No. Fine. But if you do have any other problems during the interregnum, please come and see me and I'll be happy to sort them out.

(*He leaves with the air of a man bearing up cheerfully under an enormous burden*)

Feeding the Hungry
by Bridget Foreman

NARRATOR ONE
NARRATOR TWO
BOY

The miracle of the feeding of the five thousand rarely fails to capture the imagination, not only because of its sheer scale and that twelve baskets of leftovers were collected afterwards, but primarily because of its very down-to-earth beginning. A boy is willing to share his picnic. Jesus reveals his glory to the crowd by multiplying over and over that initial act of trusting generosity. It's almost as if without the willingness of the boy, the miracle might never have happened.

Setting aside the theological purpose of the miracle, it is tempting to ask why Jesus doesn't perform miracles of this kind on an even greater scale for the thousands who die every day through lack of food. Why doesn't God appear to answer their prayers? Perhaps part of the answer for each of us, as this sketch shows, is that God wants *me* to be part of the answer.

(The sketch is started by the NARRATORS *with great warmth and confidence—as if they know all about the delightful miracle which is about to be revealed. Their twinkles of anticipation are abruptly snuffed out by the first reaction of the* BOY, *who has been discreetly visible to the audience from the start, finishing his last mouthful. He is just screwing up his sandwich bag as* TWO *turns to him)*

ONE   And in those days Jesus crossed to the far shore of the sea of Galilee.

TWO   And a great crowd of people followed him because they had seen the miraculous signs he had performed upon the sick.

ONE   And the disciples said to Jesus, 'Where shall we buy food for all these people to eat?'

TWO   But Andrew spoke up and said, 'Here is a boy with five small barley loaves and—

BOY   Oh. Sorry.

ONE   What?

BOY   I've eaten them.

TWO   You've WHAT?

BOY   I've eaten my sardine rolls.

ONE   But—you can't.

BOY   I have.

TWO   No, you don't understand—you're supposed to offer your loaves and fishes so Jesus can feed the five thousand.

BOY   Well, like I said, sorry.

ONE   Sorry?? That hardly seems adequate—

BOY   Look, it was *my* packed lunch, wasn't it? I was hungry.

TWO   But what about the crowd?

BOY   What crowd?

ONE   (*Pointing to the audience*) This crowd. The five thousand that are supposed to be being fed.

BOY   What about them?

TWO   Look you stupid little boy, it was *your* sardine rolls that were supposed to feed them.

BOY   Yeh, well *you* said it—they were my sardine rolls and I've eaten them. Anyway, if this Jesus is such a hot shot, he ought to be able to pull a gourmet meal out of thin air.

ONE   But the whole point of the story is that God wants *us* to use what we've got, however little…

TWO   To share around what he's given us…

ONE   And you have just wolfed the lot.

TWO   And the five thousand are still hungry.

    (*Pause*)

BOY   (*Leaving*) Yeh, well, like I said—sorry.

Body Language
by Nigel Forde

RAPHAEL, an archangel
HERION, a recently-appointed seraph

In my book *Theatrecraft*, I discuss the difficulty of writing on huge abstract themes, such as Redemption, Grace, The Body of Christ. So here is a sketch on the Body of Christ, the short-comings of which will point to the inherent difficulties.

The Body of Christ—that is the unity of all believers with all their different, complementary gifts, talents and characteristics—can never been seen. You can see a whole congregation; you can see tiny parts of the Body at work, but the work of the whole Body is something that can only be seen in an historical perspective or as an abstract idea. Such an idea might well be expressed in dance, but even then it would not symbolise much more than we can already understand from the expression itself.

This sketch doesn't get much further. It is little more than a mini-sermon broken into dialogue. But it has proved useful.

(*Depressed,* HERION *sits alone on stage.* RAPHAEL *enters briskly and sees him*)

RAPHAEL   Ah, hello. Herion, isn't it?

HERION   That's right. Fancy you remembering me.

RAPHAEL   Well, we archangels have to keep a check on things. I looked you up in *Who's Who in Heaven*. One of the seraphim now.

HERION   (*Gloomily*) Yeah. It's a big responsibility. Trying to keep up with the noble army of martyrs, continually crying...

RAPHAEL   You mustn't think of it like that.

HERION   Like what?

RAPHAEL   Having to keep up with the others. You're there because you're wanted.

HERION   Because somebody's wanted.

RAPHAEL   No. Because *you* are wanted. Our Lord didn't just create people and angels. He created Arthur Spendlove, Felicity Norman and John Bates, Raphael and Herion. We're all individuals.

HERION   It's just so difficult to feel important when there are thousands of others exactly like you.

RAPHAEL   Take a look at the earth again.

HERION   I'm depressed enough as it is. Sorry.

RAPHAEL   (*Directing his attention towards the audience*) Now look at all those human beings. Watch them for a minute.

HERION   Well?

RAPHAEL	What's wrong with them?
HERION	Lots of things really.
RAPHAEL	But basically?
HERION	Well some of them are aimless, short-sighted, envious, critical, frustrated, unhappy...
RAPHAEL	That'll do for a start. And they are all those things because they don't know where they fit in.
HERION	It can't just be that. Some of those people are Christians. You can't lump them in with the aimless and the frustrated.
RAPHAEL	Unfortunately the fear of God is only the beginning of wisdom. You've never been a human but you ought to try to understand them. It's easy for us. We look on the face of God every day. We know the love and the power and the glory. But what have they got? A mock-gothic refrigerator in a vandalised city square full of lost hopes, broken relationships and thwarted ambitions.
HERION	They've got the promises of Christ. Aren't they worth anything?
RAPHAEL	Everything. But they're sometimes difficult to accept when you live in a world full of broken promises.
HERION	It's harder for them than I'd realised.
RAPHAEL	Their problem is the same as yours with the rest of the seraphim.
HERION	Being one among thousands?
RAPHAEL	Trying to realise that they are important.

That Christ died for every single one of them and wants more for them than they want for themselves. (*Pause*) They have an expression down there on earth: 'Being a cog in a machine'.

HERION   That's a good one.

RAPHAEL   They don't like it. Of course, they could say one colour in a pattern or one vital organ in a body but they phrase it that way to give themselves an excuse to feel dissatisfied.

HERION   Is that what our Father means by 'the Body of Christ'? Everyone being a sort of limb?

RAPHAEL   A lip or a limb, a liver or a ligament, yes. And when they are all joined together perfectly, then Christ is seen perfectly. Naturally it doesn't work if the limbs are all in the wrong places or back to front, or the right elbow is desperately trying to use its cartilage to see in the dark.

HERION   Why should it do that?

RAPHAEL   Why should you feel unimportant among the hosts of seraphim? All the time you are yearning to be an archangel, you'll be a very bad seraph. But seraph or archangel, you're just as important as I am.

HERION   Me??!

RAPHAEL   Without you, heaven would be lacking. You may not see your own importance but God does.

HERION   I suppose so.

RAPHAEL   Just as you can see what all those people down on earth can't see. If they filled their own places they would be satisfied. But they're always hankering after something else before God is ready to give it to them. Hadn't you better get off to choir practice?

HERION   Is it that time already?

RAPHAEL   Hark!

HERION   What?

RAPHAEL   The herald angels sing.

HERION   I'd better get there—no one else knows my part!

Ninety-eight per cent Proof

TWO PEOPLE of any appropriate age or sex, chatting wherever you choose to set the conversation.

There was a professor of astrophysics, quoted by our friend and former vicar, David Watson, who not only claimed that he didn't believe in God, but that he categorically *knew* there was no God to believe in. The absurdity and arrogance of this assertion gave rise to this little sketch, which, although by no means proof of the existence of God, at least clears the ground for a sensible debate on the subject. For a more rigorous treatment, you will have to start reading Plato, Aquinas, Anselm, the Bible, etc.!

This can be staged seated, 'head to head', but it has also worked in a more casual context, such as between two stage-managers, setting the scene for the next sketch in a revue.

(A MAN *and a* WOMAN *are sitting in a café)*

MAN   Of course, getting into hospital these days isn't that easy, either.

WOMAN   What with all the waiting lists you mean?

MAN   No, it's all the forms you have to fill in. Not only do you have to know your name and address, marital status and particular blood group but there's also a little box for your beliefs.

WOMAN   So they can post them back to you afterwards.

MAN   No. On the form. A little box on the form, where you have to put down what you believe, your religion and so forth. I mean, theology isn't exactly the first thing on your mind after a car crash, is it?

WOMAN   So why do they do that, then?

MAN   Well, they want to know whether you're a Muslim or a Roman Catholic or a Methodist or something different.

WOMAN   A Melanesian Frog Worshipper. That's different.

MAN   Yeah, well they want you to be sensible about it. It's an official form.

WOMAN   So what did you put?

MAN   Nothing.

WOMAN   Oh, right. Was that because you didn't have a pen or...?

MAN   No. I just put 'nothing'.

WOMAN Oh, I see. N U double F I N. So you was like saying, 'I don't believe nothing'.

MAN Yeah. Religion's a crutch, isn't it?

WOMAN 'Course it is. (*Pause*) How do you mean... 'crutch'?

MAN For people who can't stand on their own two feet and think for themselves.

WOMAN Like drunks.

MAN Them as well. But it could apply to anybody.

WOMAN Except you, 'cos you don't believe nothing. So you wouldn't believe in taking a holiday, one man one vote, fresh air, catching murderers—

MAN No, no, no, no, obviously there are *some* things which...

WOMAN ...There wasn't room for on the form, so you put 'nothing'. Shorter.

MAN That's right. But you see they really want to know whether you believe in God, life after death, all that sort of thing—specially in hospital—which, of course, I don't believe in.

WOMAN Well, you're a clever lad, aren't you? I mean, you must know most of what there is to know in the universe. Apart from chemistry, cooking omelettes—

MAN Naturally, no one can know everything. There are bound to be a few areas of which I wouldn't be exactly 'up' on...

WOMAN ...Science, philosophy...

MAN Sure... er...

WOMAN	Politics, micro-biology…
MAN	Yeah, I dunno much about micro-biology…
WOMAN	Well…I mean I didn't know what time the bus was leaving yesterday. But in your case a person can obviously know, what…fifty per cent of all the known knowledge in the universe? Or slightly *more*?
MAN	Probably slightly less, actually.
WOMAN	Well, alright, yeah…
MAN	More like…
WOMAN	Ten per cent, maybe. (*Pause*) We could definitely be talking about two per cent, couldn't we?
MAN	Possibly.
WOMAN	That's still two per cent of all the known knowledge in the universe!
MAN	Oh, yeah. And that's a considerable amount for one human brain.
WOMAN	Especially yours. And it still leaves a further ninety-eight per cent for all the things you don't know and therefore don't believe in. Like God. He might also be in the two per cent you do know, but you haven't spotted him yet.
MAN	Well, seeing is believing, you see. I only believe in what I see.
WOMAN	That's fair enough. What do you make of the wind, love, birdsong, radar transmission, thought, the execution of Charles I–
MAN	Look, I think I've got to go now.

WOMAN   Still, we're seeing each other again tomorrow, aren't we?

MAN   I believe so, yeah.

        (*He tries to go*)

WOMAN   (*Laughs*) D'you hear what you just said...'I believe so'...D'you get it? You believe that then. (*Laughing*) But I don't believe we can actually see tomorrow, can we?

MAN   (*Laughs feebly*)

WOMAN   'I believe so'...

        (*He leaves*)

Power Failure

PONTIUS PILATE, a high-flying modern executive, governor of the Roman province of Judea.

This piece was written as one of a six-part series of fifteen-minute television monologues entitled 'The Easter Stories'. The first performance was given by Robert Duncan on BBC 1 during Holy Week in 1994. Adapted for the stage, it obviously presents a considerable challenge for an actor looking for something that goes beyond the technical demands of the other sketches in this book. It requires not only a powerful solo performance, but also an imaginative director's 'eye'. It should take place within a set which suggests a private executive washroom in a prestigious government building. The rudiments of this need to include a hand basin, a shower, mirrors, at least one entrance, a window and other bathroom furniture. As with the best set design, it is good to aim for an overall impression of the bathroom context, which combines the practical elements with those that can be stylised. You will also need good lighting and to create (for one section in particular) a quality soundtrack. With careful preparation of these production elements and a thorough exploration of the text, an excellent one-man performance is possible but it would be dangerous to attempt this sketch casually.

Pilate has been deliberately placed in the modern

era. From the seclusion of his bathroom he deals with the outside world on his mobile phone. As an aspiring politician he is constantly alert to the photo-opportunities, to the media hype and satellite broadcasts which will put a rosy glass on the precarious nature of his governorship. He has done everything in his power to turn Jerusalem's ancient Passover Festival into a huge international media event, presenting this notoriously troublesome province in a new light. As governor he intends to bask in the reflected glory of a magnificent celebration of peace, flowers, ancient religious culture and traditional arts and crafts. Caesar will be watching his performance from Rome via the satellite link-up.

His plans are very nearly de-railed by the shattering events of Good Friday, AD 33. The city, bursting with visitors, is on the verge of riot, the secular and the religious authorities are applying dangerous pressure, an innocent man is branded traitor and the sun itself is eclipsed. At the heart of these events is a personal confrontation between two men. Their encounter questions the source of real power and the very nature of truth.

(PILATE *bursts through the door. He talks urgently into a mobile phone.*)

PILATE   I can't talk to anyone—I'm not seeing anyone—
I've been up half the night. When I do meet
the press? The press conference! Grief! I've
got bags under my eyes and I'm being
beamed around the world in six hours—I'm
sweating like a pig, Publius—don't quote me
on that—just off the record—that is strictly off
the record—I thought Herod was dealing with
the Galilean busi—no, no tell them to sort
themselves out, I can't afford any more time
on this Jesus thing.

(*Slams phone down. He begins undressing for
shower and at the same time arranges the cards
for his speech around the basin*)

Why can't they ignore him like any sensible
person? It's absolutely typical, I organise a
major peace initiative, satellite link-ups, all
over the empire, try to give this city a new
image (*Seeing a headline on a card*) Jerusalem,
Garden City of the Levant—I'm proud of that—
it's catchy—Garden City—Peace. Flowers.
Plant-a-tree-in-'33. I've got proconsuls, I've
got senators from Rome, I've got governors
from Asia Minor, Bithynia, I've got the senior
Eunuch from Ethiopia...Every faith, every
culture...I've got a dirty great cedar of
Lebanon with twinkly lights flashing mes-
sages of peace and hope in twenty languages:
'Come to Jerusalem, city of your dreams, the
Feast of Passover, the Jewish Experience', but
what do they want—with all the cameras of
the world switched on? A public execution
and pictures of (*Imitating a sycophantic priest*)

113

'Governor Pilate' desperately trying to nip another revolution in the bud. Marvellous. Wonderful. (*Sourly*) The festive spirit.

(*He tests the water but it is boiling hot—he burns himself*)

Aaah! (*He turns to scan his notes*) Your excellency, the Imperial Ambassador, Nobles, Lords, Ladies, men of Judea...change that... citizens of Judea...change that...citizens of...this province...um...for this brief moment we find ourselves at the three cornerstones of civilisation...three cornerstones? ...um, the apex...no!...The great cornerstone...A cornice of the apex, no!...Sounds like corner...um we find ourselves facing a huge...corner...challenge...I therefore bid you...friends of his august Majesty...fellow beneficiaries of his divine favour...that's good...of our most excellent Caesar...I call you Caesar's friends...welcome (*Stepping towards the shower boldly*) Welcome to Jerusalem!

(*Phone rings*)

I can't talk now. I can't talk. I'm in the shower, I'm preparing my speech—*this* is urgent. Nothing else is urgent. Don't have anything to do with...oh, not you as well...what's the matter with everybody? I have no intention of having anything else to do with Jesus... There...happy? Bye bye. Yes, I had a bad night...yes, we've all suffered much...this night! For God's sake, Flavia, you and your dreams. Go and talk to your therapist. I won't...I won't...I won't do anything I'll regret...I won't touch him...39 lashes? Yes,

I'll admit, I did have to teach him a lesson...A public flogging? Public relations, Flavia. That's what this weekend is all about. There's going to be no death, no executions, no revolutions, just lots of flowers. And people shaking hands. The breaking down of barriers. And the only people who are going to get hurt are those who stand in the way of the peace initiative...Flavia...Flavia...Flavia... my darling you are way out of control.

(Phone down. He buries his face in a towel for a moment. The phone rings again)

If you say so, if you say so, fine, he's the son of God—I don't have a problem with that *(Pause)*—I know they do *(Pause)*—I told them to release him. There's a custom—Governor's privilege—at Passover. Free any prisoner. Pick a prisoner for Passover. I told them to free him. I am not, repeat not, going to execute an innocent man, even if he is a lunatic, even if he calls himself the son of...*(Pause)* Did they?? *(Appalled)* King of the Jews...and I am not Caesar's friend if...*(grabs shirt and tie)* I'm coming down.

(He leaves abruptly as the lights fade for a few seconds. Pause. The door bursts open. This time PILATE *half collapses against the basin...outside, faintly, we hear the roar of a crowd)*

My kingdom is not of this world...he stands there, he's dirty, he's filthy, he's dripping with blood...but he talks of kingdoms...he's looking at me, he talks to me about power *(Imitating his own public performance)* 'Don't you realise I have the power of life and death over you?...He's silent, he's staring, straight

115

through me, and he says, 'You have no power...No power...which has not been given from above...' So I say to him, 'So you're a king then?' More silence. More staring. Like he's waiting for me to say something, to give an account of myself. I mean, who's on trial here?...(*Splashes his face*) I've got to get ready...It's too hot in here, stifling. I haven't even had a shower. I must get my head together. (*Taking shirt off*) I can't breathe in here. (*He opens a window. The roar of the crowd intensifies*) Listen to them...listen to them...who's on trial? (*He looks down. Softly*) Behold the man!...Even my centurions keep their distance...he just stands there...'the reason for my coming into the world is to bear witness to the truth.' (*He looks away*) What is truth?

(*As he continues to undress he catches sight of his own reflection. A long meaningful gaze between himself and his reflection. He looks down. He sees a tiny speck of blood on the cuff. He looks up*)

I asked him straight—what is truth? And then silence. Those eyes.

(*Suddenly washes off blood furiously. Waving through the window and shouting*)

See, I am washing my hands of this—I am washing my hands of all of you—see! Clean! Clean!

(*He grabs the phone*)

Publius...(*Silence*) Just do it. And Publius...I want that body down off the cross before sunset.

(The lights fade again briefly. As they return, PILATE *emerges from the shower—a towel tied round his waist and another flung over his shoulder. Almost a toga. He gazes into the mirror)*

'Relax, breathe deeply, look yourself in the eye and say "I feel okay about myself." ' *(Breathes deeply)* Clench fists, relax. Clench fists, relax. Breathe deeply. 'There is nothing you cannot do if you put your mind to it.' I believe in myself. I believe in me. I am comfortable with myself. This is what I am. This is me. I like me. 'Remember you have the resources.' *(Silence. He is dabbing on aftershave)* I have the resources. I have the power. 'Give a present to yourself every day and find something new you really like about yourself.' *(Pause)* It is extremely rare for me to condemn an innocent man to death. *(Pause)* To the best of my knowledge I have only done it once. *(Pause)* Today. *(He breathes deeply)* There will be mistakes along the way. I have crucified an innocent man but it was a learning experience. I am not responsible. I am not wholly responsible. I am responsible for saving the lives of many women and children today from a futile revolution that could have destroyed the entire nation. I have saved the nation. I have saved lives. I have absolutely no regrets. It is negative to focus on the past. This is not a resigning matter. *(Silence. He dries his hair)* What is truth? It depends on your point of view. It depends on your life experience. Exactly. Precisely. Truth? *(He dries his hair more vigorously)* What is it? What is it? What is truth? What is truth? What is truth? Is there anyone in the whole universe who has

117

the answer to that!! The right to say what truth is!? (*Slams towel down. Silence*) 'It's okay to be angry.' I feel comfortable with my anger. I feel... it's all right to be angry. 'Remember, you have the power!!' I have the power! 'Direct your anger to the source...' yes... (*turning to the window*) it's you... it's you... it's you out there... IT'S YOU... it's you...!! Hanging on the cross... you think I've hurt you... look what you've done to *me*... YOU ARE RESPONSIBLE!!

(*The lights blow. A few seconds later, the emergency lights flicker and die*)

(*In the blackout, we hear a powerful sound montage of* PILATE's *words; echoes of the previous monologue, overlapping, fading, multiplying*)

(*Speaking to Publius on the mobile phone*) I can't afford any more time on this Jesus thing!

(*Murmuring to himself in the mirror*) Why can't they ignore him like any sensible person?

(*Shouting to his wife*) I am not, repeat not, going to execute an innocent man!...

(*Reflecting on his meeting with Christ*) Don't you realise that I have the power of life or death over you?...

(*Repeating the words of Jesus, whispering them, incredulous*) No power... which has not been given from above. (*Echoing*) From above... above...

The reason for my coming into the world is to bear witness to the truth... what is truth?

(*Yelling through the window*) See I am washing

118

my hands of this–I am washing my hands of all of you!

(*To himself*) What is truth?...

(*Dimly we see* PILATE *alone, a tiny figure huddled in the dark*)

(*The voice continues*) I am not responsible.

(*Then suddenly, ten* PILATES *are asking the question*) What is truth?...

(*Furiously shouting*) IS THERE ANYONE IN THE WHOLE UNIVERSE WHO HAS A RIGHT TO SAY WHAT TRUTH IS?...!

(*Finally the voices fade, echoing, dissolving, merging*) Truth...Truth...Truth...

(*The dim light grows.* PILATE *is still cowering, head in hands. Phone rings. It rings for a long time before he moves. At last he picks up the phone*)

Yes...Yes...Yes...Arimithea?...(*Pause*)   I don't want to talk to anyone from the Sanhedrin...(*Silence*) I see. Put him on... mm-hmm...you want me to give you the body of your king...why? (*Silence*) Are you out of your mind? (*Silence*) You didn't have the courage to beg for his life (*incredulous*) so now you are begging for his corpse. (*He shakes his head, half laughing. Silence*) Take it. (*He flicks the switch*)

(*Talking to himself softly, he dresses quickly. Full lights suddenly snap on*)

(*Sarcastically*) Oh thank you. Normal service...(*stretching out the words*) resuuuumed! Thank you very, very much.

119

(*Muzak plays from a tannoi.* PILATE *is psyching himself up as he dresses. Regaining control. He puts on watch. Checks the time*)

Right.

(*He assumes his public role with growing self assurance. The troubles of the last few hours are brushed aside with occasional whistles through the teeth, deep breaths, a hand smoothing a hair into place, a sigh, an adjustment of his collar. His dressing reaches a basic state of readiness before final details—tie, cufflinks, shoelaces, flower in the button hole—to be accomplished during the final phone call. Catching sight of his speech cards he begins again*)

Your excellency, The Imperial Ambassador, Nobles, Lords, Ladies, Citizens of Judea, it is my...(*Coughs, clears throat unsuccessfully. Fills a glass and gargles.*) Your excellency, The Imperial Am... (*Checks watch and dials on the mobile*) Publius...Yeah...I'll be there in ten minutes...fine...power back on? I'm not interested Publius...You're the press officer. Just put it down to freak weather conditions...okay? Yeah...yeah...so when do we go live...yeah...and everyone in the press room should have a button hole. I want flowers, lots of flowers. What? You've got what? No, no, no, no more priests. Look, just get them out of the foyer...not one priest in shot please. Yep. A priest free zone, Publius. You've got it. Guards. Who wants Guards?? (*Sighing with infinite patience*) They want a guard. And why is that? And why is that Publius? Am I missing something? Am I missing a local custom, practised over thousands of years, the ritual guarding of completely dead people—in case they suddenly decide to pop out to the shops!! What am I missing here? Apart from one single human being who has the vaguest, infinitesimal approximation to a brain! A prophecy, well…He said…(*Changing his tone*) He said that did he? Are you sure about this? My wife…my wife told you. Anyone else? My great-aunt, my grandmother? (*Silence*) Oh I see. It doesn't matter who said it because the prophecy is now public knowledge. I am trying to arrange an international peace conference, tell the whole world about the amazing stability of Roman rule in Palestine and our extraordinary grip on local affairs, but I am the only one in this entire province who is—patently—obviously—a complete IGNORAMUS. (*Sighs*) Guard the tomb, Publius. Guard the tomb. Sign the warrant, let them have the massed bands of the tenth legion and sixty whirling dervishes dancing on his grave. It's all the same to me. You can't be too careful when it comes to burying the son of God. Let's be thorough, let's be efficient.

(*He slams the phone down*)

Three days…

(*He shakes his head. He smiles. He mechanically washes his hands one more time. He turns to the audience*)

Your excellency, Imperial Ambassador, my Lords, Ladies, Citizens of this province… Welcome to this great festival, welcome to the

121

new order of peace and prosperity...I apologise for some of the technical problems we've been having...a few disturbances in the street and a temporary loss of power. A few problems with power...But all is back to normal, I can assure you. And we are doing our best in difficult circumstances. I am sure many people will identity with me when I say that the phrase 'we are doing our best' is no mere cliché but contains a valuable message for the world.

(It is as if a rehearsal to himself in the mirror has now become a keynote international broadcast)

We have reached a moment in our civilisation of which we can be proud...justifiably proud...a moment of peace...Peace is hard to find in this troubled world and everywhere it is threatened...above all by the past...we must put the past behind us...we must learn to think the best of ourselves and not to dwell on...our mistakes...which often turn out to be...in hindsight...steps on the road to maturity, to peace...of mind—For that is where peace begins. Inside. We must look deep inside ourselves where to tell you the truth—the truth is...er...we have untapped resources, we have power...

(Lights fade to black)

The Daniel Rap
by Bridget Foreman

NARRATOR

SATRAPS

KING DARIUS

DANIEL

LIONS

ANGEL

A strong drummer is an almost essential requirement for a successful and energetic performance of this sketch. It must be fast-moving and physical. Obviously the cast can be expanded or reduced to suit your company: this arrangement is only a suggestion. Similarly it is the off-beat interjections that will give the performance much of its colour.

NARRATOR	I wanna tell ya a story 'bout a man called Dan,
	He lived a long time ago in a far away land.
	He was smart, he was wise, but it all began
	Because right from the start he was
ALL	(*beat*) God's man!
NARRATOR	Daniel had a job, he worked for the king,
	He helped and advised him with everything,
	The king could see he was sensible,
	In no time Dan was indispensable.
	There were other guys who worked for the king
	Dan's meteoric rise set them a-thinking:
SATRAPS	The way this Dan has got to the top
	Gets right up our noses, it's got to stop.
	Let's think of a way we can bring him down
	So he'll no longer be number one in town!
NARRATOR	So they set their minds to a difficult task
	Turned to each other and began to ask:
SATRAPS	How can we frame this Daniel guy
	And make ourselves look sweeter than pie?
	Doesn't lie, doesn't swear, doesn't cheat the books
	Doesn't steal, doesn't even give us dirty looks.
	We've racked our brains for even one complaint
	But to no avail—the man's a saint! Aha!

NARRATOR	And then they remembered the thing about Dan Was first and foremost he was
ALL	(*beat*) God's man!
NARRATOR	They had an idea for a
SATRAPS	new decree: For a month it is a crime to bend the knee Or pray or worship anyone else Except–what genius–the king himself!
NARRATOR	The king thought this was a
KING	cool plan!
NARRATOR	He forgot that Daniel was
NARRATOR & DANIEL	(*beat*) God's man!
NARRATOR	Now Daniel carried on in his usual way, Praying to God three times each day. He opened his window, got down on his knees And his worship was carried to God on the breeze. Now his enemies saw him at prayer one day, Went to the king and gave the game away
SATRAPS	O King, you remember that new decree– Who should we worship? The king answered
KING	Me!
SATRAPS	Well, King, we don't like to tell tales outa school

But that pet of yours, Daniel, has broken
    the rule
Now if you remember, the small print
    states
That those who flout what the law
    dictates
Should pay the price for being a sinner
And end their days as the lions' dinner
    (*Roar*)

NARRATOR   Now the king was troubled in his
    thoughtless way
He'd forgotten how much Daniel loved
    to pray
And he turned his mind to how to save
    Dan,
He liked him—even if he was

ALL   (*beat*) God's man!

NARRATOR   He studied the books—one thing was
    revealed;
The decree was law—couldn't be
    repealed.
So Daniel was fetched by those jealous
    men,
And thrown straight into the lions' den.

(DAN *gives a loud cry as if falling down a
hole*)

NARRATOR   As the king saw Dan go into the lair
He sent up his own little kingly prayer.
He prayed that when it came to the
    crunch,
Dan wouldn't be the lions' lunch.
the king went to bed—he couldn't sleep a
    wink,
He couldn't read his book or eat or

drink.
All he could see when he closed his eyes
Was the lions tucking in to Daniel with
    fries.
Meanwhile back at the lions' lair,
Dan was putting in some serious prayer.

DANIEL   HEEEEELLLLLPPPPPPP!!!

NARRATOR   God looked down and he saw poor Dan,
He said 'Hang on a minute, that's

ALL   (*beat*) MY MAN!

NARRATOR   What I need right now is an angel who's
    fast—
I don't know how long poor Daniel will
    last.'
So he picked up the phone, sent an
    urgent fax:
'Dan's on the menu as lion snacks!'
Off flew the angel, swift and speedy,
Hoping the lions weren't feeling greedy.
He flew right into the lions' lair,
And said to the cats, 'Just hold it right
    there!

(*He shows a business card and reads off it to
the lions*) G.O.D.

I'd advise you to do nothing hasty.'
The cats were disappointed: Dan looked
    tasty.

(DAN *and the* ANGEL *greet each other with
a series of hand-slaps and street calls*)

But the angel hadn't finished: he turned
to the lions:
'Now just behave, I don't want no
    violence

Hide your teeth, put your claws in
    mittens,
Let me see you in the corner, purring
    like kittens.'
The king was overjoyed to see Dan alive,
He said:

KING   I didn't think that you would survive.

NARRATOR   Daniel told the king

DANIEL   My God is great.
            I knew he wouldn't let me be lions' bait.

NARRATOR   The king was stunned:

KING   Your God is amazin'
           Daniel, teach me how to get praisin'!!

(*All break to a short burst of the Hallelujah
Chorus*)

NARRATOR   And the king he issued a new decree:

ALL   Worship the God who sets you free.

NARRATOR   He even saved Daniel from the lions' den
           That's why we're proud to be

ALL   (*beat*) God's men!

Daniel in the Lions' Den

a puppet show

NARRATOR

TWO LIONS

LADY, from the board of film censors

DANIEL

KING DARIUS

MAURICE THE MEANY, the Grand Vizier

MR SPRINGE, his sidekick.

Riding Lights has not had great experience of using puppets despite their perennial popularity with children. As *Sesame Street* and *The Muppets* have proved so effectively, they can also be highly entertaining for adults. This script was originally performed in the streets of York from a brightly-striped puppet theatre, mounted on top of a pony trap. It may encourage others to rediscover the skill and fun of puppetry in a variety of contexts including the Family Service.

Scene 1

(*Music*)

NARRATOR Ladies and gentlemen, MGM pictures presents... (*MGM circle goes on, plus lion*) THE STORY OF DANIEL IN THE LIONS' DEN.

(LION *roars*)

LADY On behalf of the British Board of Film Censors I certify this film suitable for family viewing (*She hangs 'U' certificate on front of puppet theatre.* LION *eats her and replaces it with 'Cert 18'*)

NARRATOR Starring Daniel, the hero (*cheer*): a good man who feared God. And king Darius–sometimes good (*cheer*) and sometimes bad (*boo*). And the Grand Vizier–Maurice the Meany (*boo*)–a thoroughly bad man. And his secretary, Springe (*boo*)–totally utterly and irredeemably bad. No-one would go near him, not even his mother. And last, but not least–THE BRITISH LIONS!! (*The lions enter and roar. All the other characters exeunt screaming*) Every day Daniel prayed to God:

Scene 2

DANIEL God, there are many people in this country who don't put their trust in you–please protect me from my enemies.

NARRATOR Yes!! Because Daniel had lots of enemies who–

130

LION A	(*Cough*) Hey!
LION B	(*Cough*)
LION A	Hey, when are we on?
NARRATOR	Not yet, not yet!
LION B	Give us a look at the script!
NARRATOR	Why?
LION B	We've got to learn our lions (*Raucous laughter*).
NARRATOR	Get off! You're on later. (*Exeunt LIONS*) So—as I was saying—
LION B	When?
NARRATOR	LATER!!
LION B	Thanks boss.
LION A	Okay boss (*Exeunt*).
NARRATOR	Sssh! Look who's coming now! It's Maurice the Meany and Mr Spring (sss!).

Scene 3

MAURICE	All is complete for my plan to become the most powerful man in the kingdom.
SPRINGE	Yes, Master.
MAURICE	Except for one thing!
SPRINGE	What is that, Master?
MAURICE	Daniel!! He is the favourite of king Darius. What are we going to do? Think, Springe, think!!
	(*They think*)

SPRINGE	Ah ha!!
MAURICE	What is it, Springe?
SPRINGE	I have it, Master!
MAURICE	What's that?
SPRINGE	Chicken pox.
MAURICE	Fool. I have a better idea. Come this way. (*Exit*) Aaargh!
SPRINGE	Mind the stairs, Master.
	(*Exit*)
NARRATOR	And this was the plan. They went to the king and persuaded him to pass a law that everyone was to worship king Darius and that if anyone was caught worshipping God they would be thrown to the lions!
LION A	That's us!
NARRATOR	Not yet.
LION B	We're the lions.
NARRATOR	There's one more scene yet.
LION A	Oh please, cut it out.
LION B	GO ON...
LION A	Please, can I do my roar now?
NARRATOR	Not now, Henry.
LION A	Go on, it's a great roar. It's my best roar.
NARRATOR	Get off!!
LION B	Just a quick roar?
NARRATOR	NO! (*Grabbing a gun*) GET OFF!!

LION A	Yes, boss.
LION B	Sure, boss.
LION A	Take it easy, boss.
NARRATOR	And so—
LIONS	Sorry boss.
	(*Exeunt* LIONS)
NARRATOR	And so Daniel, who trusted in God, carried on praying to God, law or no law about worshipping king Darius.

Scene 4

DANIEL	Dear God, help me not to be afraid to worship you whatever anyone else says.
MAURICE	Nyha!! Caught you in the act!! Mr Springe, have you got the photographs?
SPRINGE	No, Master.
MAURICE	You blithering idiot, Springe.
SPRINGE	I've got some postcards of Margate, Master.
MAURICE	Fool! Fetch the king.
SPRINGE	Yes, Master. (*Exit*) Aaargh!!
MAURICE	Mind the stairs, Spring.
	(SPRINGE *re-enters with the* KING)
	Aha! Your Majesty—we have caught Daniel breaking the law you made.
SPRINGE	You must throw him to the lions.

133

LIONS	(*Making a sudden appearance*) YEAH–THAT'S US!!
KING	Oh–Oh dear–but I like Daniel. He's my best friend.
MAURICE	A law is a law, your Majesty.
KING	Oh dear–well–we'd better throw him to the lions, then.
	(MEANIES *cheer. Exeunt*)

Scene 5

NARRATOR	And so Daniel was thrown into the lions' den. LIONS!!…LIONS??…LIONS!!??
LIONS	Yeah?
NARRATOR	You're on.
LION A	What now?
NARRATOR	Yes.
LION B	What do you mean, 'on'?
NARRATOR	It's your scene.
LION A	Did we miss the cue?
NARRATOR	Yes.
LION A	Oh sorry boss, we were down at the Red Lion (*Raucous laughter*).
NARRATOR	Get on with it.
LION B	(*Producing menu*) Ah, Henry, what's on this menu?
LION A	Leg on toast (*laugh*).
LION B	Daniel fingers (*laugh*).

LION A	Daniel with arm and sauce...arm and sauce!! (*laugh*).
LION B	Tongue salad (*laugh*), followed by?
LION A	Spare ribs!
LION A	And Daniel burgers (*can hardly contain himself*). What's for afters?
LION A	Daniel surprise.
LION B	When we leap up on him?
LION A	Yeah, otherwise known as CAT AND MOUSSE!!
LION B	What else?
LION A	Raspberry rip-up.
LION B	And finally...knees and biscuits!!
	(*They fall about*)
NARRATOR	But Daniel prayed to the Lord, and God shut the mouth of the lions.
LIONS	For what we are about to receive may the—ulp!! (*2 hands stifle them*).
NARRATOR	And along came king Darius in the morning and shouted:
KING	Daniel!! DANIEL!!
DANIEL	Yes?
KING	Are you all right?
DANIEL	I'm fine.
KING	How are the lions?
DANIEL	Fine—how are yours?
KING	Fine.

DANIEL	But, they are a bit hungry.
KING	(*Knowingly, towards audience*) What shall we give them to eat?
DANIEL	Um...well...
KING	What about...Maurice the Meany and Mr Springe!
	(*Chase and general crunching up of baddies*)
OLD CHORUS	(*Sung by two lions*) Dare to be a Daniel Dare to stand alone Dare to have a purpose firm Dare to make it known
	(DANIEL *comes on and they sing again. Just before they try and eat him, their mouths are shut. He pats their heads. Purring and general affection. They take a bow*)
	(*Exeunt*)

News of the Word

Two Mimes:
NEWSPRINT
and PROPHET

This is not the first sketch to exploit the idea of visual dialogue between news vendors' slogans. Nevertheless, it is a welcome variation in style within an evening of sketches. The choreography of the movement and the quality of the props is all important. So too is the timing with which each slogan is introduced into the conversation. The whole sequence will benefit from a continuous musical backing.

NEWSPRINT is selling newspapers from a stand. He is dressed in clothes decorated with newspaper. PROPHET is colourfully dressed, selling a stack of Bibles from a similar stand next to NEWSPRINT. They communicate via slogans written on large pads of paper attached to the front of their stands, ripping them off one at a time as the script indicates.

(NEWSPRINT *folds up one of his papers, laughs at* PROPHET *and flicks scornfully through one of her Bibles. He tosses it on the ground. She picks it up and replaces it carefully on the stack. He points with relish at his first slogan*)

NEWSPRINT	PROPHET
1. THE DAILY GRIND.	
	2. GLAD TIDINGS.
3. ALL THE LATEST SCANDAL! VERY TASTY! VERY EXCITING!	
	4. RUBBISH! THERE'S NOTHING NEW UNDER THE SUN. The Bible
5. CHRISTIANITY HAS NOTHING TO SAY, ADMITS PREACHER.	
	6. WE'LL SOON SEE ABOUT THAT, SUNSHINE.
7. WAR OF WORDS! NEWSVENDOR VERY CONFIDENT.	
	8. GOD OPPOSES THE PROUD–OFFICIAL. James 4
9. MORE AND MORE HORRIFYING DISASTERS!!! CLOSE-UP COLOUR PICS!!!	

10. STALE BUNS,
    MATE. WARS,
    EARTHQUAKES,
    FAMINES, DIS-
    EASES ALL
    FORECAST YEARS
    AGO.

    Luke 21

(NEWSPRINT *is getting
more agitated. He is
desperate not to be
made to look a fool*)

11. LOTS MORE DIS-
    ASTERS! PLUS
    £50,000 TO BE
    WON!!!

12. GUTTER PRESS
    SINKS TO ALL-
    TIME LOW.

(NEWSPRINT *threatens*
PROPHET)

13. BIBLE FREAK TOLD
    TO WATCH IT OR
    ELSE.

    (*The sense of competi-
    tion builds up*)

14. BIG BRITISH
    ASSETS COMPANY
    SHARE OFFER!
    SPEND! SPEND!
    SPEND!

15. SPEND NOW–PAY LATER: MAN GAINS WHOLE WORLD BUT LOSES SOUL.

Matthew 16

16. RECORD GOLD RESERVES! BANKS VERY HAPPY.

17. GET TREASURE IN HEAVEN! GIVE TO THE POOR.

Mark 10

18. TRIBAL SLAUGH-TER DILEMMA: THE WORLD WAITS.

19. DILEMMA SOLVED YEARS AGO IN SERMON ON MOUNT (of Peace-makers).

20. CRISIS WORSENS IN MIDDLE EAST!

21. YEP, TROUBLE IN STORE FOR ALL THOSE WHO NEG-LECT JUSTICE!

Luke 11

(NEWSPRINT *is getting mad*)

22. CAN'T YOU FIND ANYTHING EXCIT-ING AND ORIGINAL?

23. SMARTASS MUST GO!

140

24. VENDETTA! CAR-
NAGE, RAPE,
MURDER, CRIME,
VICAR, SEX,
MURDER, SEX,
ETC., ETC.

25. FORGIVENESS!
FAR BETTER RES-
ULTS!

Luke 6

26. 'RELIGIOUS'
ENTERTAINER IN
TAX DODGE
SCANDAL.

27. GOD OR MONEY–
THE CHOICE IS
YOURS!

Luke 16

28. BUZZ OFF OR GET
DONE IN–THE
CHOICE IS YOURS.

29. LOVE NEVER
ENDS.

St Paul

(NEWSPRINT *finally
goes beserk and stran-
gles* PROPHET)

30. MAD NEWS
VENDOR BATTERS
BIBLE MANIAC TO
DEATH.

(NEWSPRINT *turns back to where* PROPHET's *body is lying in front of her stand. He sneaks a look at her next slogan which reads*)

31. OK, YOU WIN, BUT REMEMBER...

   (*He turns over the final page*)

32. MY WORDS WILL NEVER PASS AWAY.

   Jesus

Pharaoh's Dream

THE BUTLER, ageing, camp, reinstated to his position after a spell in prison

PHARAOH, ruler of Egypt, locked into the 'sixties' peace-love-and-drugs culture

JOSEPH, young, Hebrew, imprisoned unjustly.

This is simply one episode in the story of Joseph as recorded in the book of Genesis. In fact, it isn't *as recorded*, of course, since imagination has been at work, embroidering characters which are otherwise rather palely drawn in the biblical account. If you happen to need a sketch on Pharaoh's Dream and how God begins to make 'all things work together for good' in the life of a somewhat unlikeable young man, you are in luck. On the other hand, this piece may serve as an illustration of how simple dramatisation, with colourful characters, can replace a reading from Scripture. Some might also feel inspired to write the other scenes in this same story and so create their own 'Joseph Soap'.

(As the scene opens in PHARAOH's *bedroom,* THE BUTLER *is tip-toeing around, clearing glasses, turning out lights and making final preparations for bed.* PHARAOH *is already snoring)*

BUTLER   Now it happened one night the Great Pharaoh of Egypt had a dream. *(Sighs)* He's always having dreams. Which in my view is not really very surprising. Well, look at him.

PHARAOH   *(Waking in panic)* Ah–uh–ah–aaahhh!! Hey man! I just had a really bad trip, man. Hey, whoa! Gimme air!! Steward! Hey! People!

BUTLER   Sssh! Shushshushshush! Whoa–wo–wo! It's alright. Would the Great Pharaoh care for a little something to soothe his nerves?

PHARAOH   What's that?

BUTLER   Something from the cellars, perhaps? A potion? A preparation?

PHARAOH   Get me a magician?

BUTLER   A magician. A magician from the cellars? Is there something troubling his Exalted Greatness?

PHARAOH   Listen man, I dreamt I was standing by the river Nile, okay? Standing there really cool, just mellowing out in my mind. And then the river, like, gave birth to seven cows, man.

BUTLER   Seven cows. I see. Yes. Uh-humn.

PHARAOH   Yeah. These animals were like, huge... beautiful colours, so fat and sleek and they came up out of the river and they touched

144

me man, in my soul. You dig that? I loved those big-eyed beasts feeding in the rushes.

BUTLER   I see.

PHARAOH   And then, you know what happened then?

BUTLER   I daren't think.

PHARAOH   Seven more cows came out of the river, man. Like wow! Hea-vee! Only these weren't so heavy, no, they were like, lean and mean and hungry, man. They gave me bad vibes, man. Bad, hungry vibes. Like they were so hungry they ate and ate and ate and they ate up my seven beautiful fat cows feeding in the rushes. All gone, man. A hole in my soul.

BUTLER   Most distressing, your Supreme Greatness.

PHARAOH   Get me a magician, man. Some wise egghead to explain this to me, man. 'Cos, like dreams are really cool, you know, they can mean things like the future and that, man. I mean, what do *you* think those cows could mean, man?

BUTLER   I would say, with the greatest respect, they could mean that your Shining Eminence, er 'went too heavy on the cheese last night, man'. Dairy products–very unwise in a hot climate. No wonder you're seeing cows.

PHARAOH   But listen, don't give me this. 'Cos I dreamed again, man and it all happened a second time.

BUTLER	Dear me.
PHARAOH	Not with cows—with, like, corn. Seven fat ears and seven thin ears of corn.
BUTLER	What *did* you have to eat last night?
PHARAOH	The thin ears ate up the big ears.
BUTLER	I beg your pardon?
PHARAOH	Yeah, it was weird. I gotta have my magicians, my wise men of Egypt.
BUTLER	Ooh! I shouldn't bother with all them at this time of night. Ooh no! With all their dusty old papyri and alligator droppings. Complete waste of time and the smell will hang around in here for weeks. No, no. I've just remembered the perfect man for you.
PHARAOH	Hey man, you gotta man for me, man?
BUTLER	Yes, and as it happens, he *is* in the cellars! Well, the dungeons really. I met him there a few years ago and he interpreted a dream of mine. Extremely accurately as it turned out. I'd forgotten all about him. Nice young man called Joseph. A Hebrew I think. Said I'd be restored to favour as your chief cup-bearer. And I was. Thanks to your Merciful Effervescence.
PHARAOH	Hey man. He sounds like the business. Wheel him right in. Now.
BUTLER	Of course.
	(*He shouts off stage for* JOSEPH *the Hebrew*)
	It might be wise to give him a bath first. I didn't find the dungeons exactly spot-

146

less...Ooh! My goodness, here he is. That was quick.

(*He holds a handkerchief over his nose as* JOSEPH *enters. The* BUTLER *leaves*)

PHARAOH   Hey, man. Joseph, right?

JOSEPH   Right.

PHARAOH   Listen, Jo-baby. I've had this far out dream, son, and they tell me you're, like, into dreams, right?

JOSEPH   Well—

PHARAOH   Like you can say what they mean?

JOSEPH   Well, I can't do anything. I don't count. But God will give Pharaoh a favourable answer.

PHARAOH   He will? That's cool, man. I'm waiting. Hit me.

JOSEPH   Well, the dream of the cows and the dream of the corn are one and the same. God is showing Pharaoh what he is going to do. The seven fat cows and seven full ears of corn are seven years of plentiful harvest. But they will be followed by seven years of famine which will exhaust the land of Egypt so that the years of plenty will be forgotten.

PHARAOH   That's heavy, man. That's really heavy—so what should I do? I need my best men on this—what do you think?

JOSEPH   You need to choose an intelligent, wise governor immediately to reserve one fifth of the harvest of each plentiful year and

147

store it in the towns, under guard, so that it will be there during the years of famine, and the land will not be destroyed by this impending disaster.

PHARAOH   I like that. I like it. I like your mind, son. It gives off the Spirit of God.

JOSEPH   Thank you. Glad to be a help, your Eminence.

PHARAOH   Oh yeah. You will be. 'Cos you just got the job.

A Slight Twinge

MAN, dressed for work in the City
HIS CONSCIENCE, looking not dissimilar to Moses.

So often we misread the ten commandments. We tend
to think of them as ten links in a chain to a heavy ball
restricting our freedom. Little by little we file away at
the links that prevent our escape. How different they
look if we read them as ten characteristics of a perfect
world which God has created for our enjoyment. A
world where we will not worship many gods, where
we will not steal, kill, commit adultery or tell lies. A
world full of so many delightful possibilities. The
more we continue to think of ourselves as trapped, not
liberated by God's laws, the more we will seek to
amend them. This sketch might have been called 'The
Ten Amendments'.

(*The* MAN *is in his office.* CONSCIENCE *enters, carrying a heavy briefcase containing two stone tablets*)

CONSCIENCE   You wanted to see me sir?

MAN   Yes, sit down, Conscience. It's time that you and I did some straight talking.

CONSCIENCE   What's this all about?

MAN   It seems to me, my Conscience, that your attitude has been increasingly negative towards me recently. What do you say to that?

CONSCIENCE   Well, sir, that's not what I've been–

MAN   Yes it *has*! You've been moralising, difficult, and pulling some very long and disapproving faces. Sooner or later there's going to be some serious trouble.

CONSCIENCE   I want to avoid any trouble, that's why I've–

MAN   Conscience?

CONSCIENCE   Yes?

MAN   Don't interrupt. You see, it's symptomatic of your whole attitude. Interruptions. Interferences. 'Watch out for this.' 'Don't do that.' Sticking your nose in where it's not at all welcome. You have to move with the times, Conscience. We're not on Mount Sinai now, you know. It's no longer a simple case of a few 'Thou Shalt Nots'. Things are subtler, more delicate, these days. Much more a case of, 'Thou shalt diligently weigh up all the changing moral com-

150

	plexities of a fast-moving modern society thereunto.' I'm too old for commandments, Conscience. It's like being back at school. All I need from you are a few sensible adult guidelines.
CONSCIENCE	Is that *adult* as in films, sir?
MAN	That's the sort of thing, yes.
CONSCIENCE	But the issues seem perfectly clear to me.
MAN	That is because you are out of date, Conscience. You seem boneheadedly incapable of dragging yourself into the twentieth century.
CONSCIENCE	There are lots of other issues I'm keen to develop, sir. Third world concern, race relations, inner city deprivation, nuclear waste, investments in repressive dictatorships–but it's you who are stuck on all the old chestnuts!
MAN	I'm sick and tired of your smug, know-it-all attitude. Take last week.
CONSCIENCE	At the golf club?
MAN	Yes.
CONSCIENCE	(*Referring to tablet*) Old chestnuts number 10. Thou shalt not covet.
MAN	Yes, yes. Number 10, number 10. I know all about number 10. I don't need you to tell me. But item 10 says nothing about Gerald and Rowena's new-look Mercedes executive saloon, for goodness sake!

CONSCIENCE	(*Reading Rubric*) 'Nor thy neighbour's ox, nor his ass'. It's the modern equivalent, sir.
MAN	What is?
CONSCIENCE	The Mercedes Executive Saloon. It's a kind of turbo ox.
MAN	(*After a pause*) You've got no idea, have you, Conscience?
CONSCIENCE	Sorry, sir?
MAN	Where would civilisation be without a sense of advance? Moving ahead to the bigger and the better?
CONSCIENCE	And the more expensive.
MAN	That has nothing to do with it.
CONSCIENCE	You've thought about nothing else all week!
MAN	I'm simply appreciating a technological milestone. Of course, it's wasted on a rich nerd like Gerald.
CONSCIENCE	But you already have two cars.
MAN	Man needs goals to aim at. A better standard of living is a noble aspiration. To aspire is not covetousness.
CONSCIENCE	It's probably closer to idolatry in your case. That's old chestnut number 1, by the way. 'You shall have no other gods before me.' That includes what you drive around in.
MAN	I don't want to discuss this with you,

	Conscience. I don't really want to discuss anything with you.
CONSCIENCE	Not even Stephanie?
MAN	Why do you mention her?
CONSCIENCE	Numbers 10 and 7, sir, the one about committing adultery.
MAN	My dear Conscience, there is absolutely no danger–
CONSCIENCE	But you're a married man!
MAN	And Stephanie needs a shoulder to cry on at the moment.
CONSCIENCE	Not *that* late at night, she doesn't.
MAN	Stephanie is my PA. Our relationship is well in control and strictly between ourselves.
CONSCIENCE	Thou shalt not get found out, you mean?
MAN	You've been overworking, Conscience. You're becoming dangerously over-sensitive. Hysterical. It's not good for you.
CONSCIENCE	Too many of your late nights.
MAN	Yes. You're tired, you see.
CONSCIENCE	I can't relax.
MAN	You must relax.
CONSCIENCE	The pangs of guilt.
MAN	You need to sleep. And if you can't sleep, then you must take something to help you sleep. (*Pouring a drink*) This should do the trick.

CONSCIENCE   What is it?

MAN   No need to worry about that. (*Reading from a packet of pills*) 'Dissolve the tablets'. (*He chuckles enigmatically*) Yes, wouldn't I just like to. (*He drops some into the glass*) There, that should deal with those pangs of guilt. Now drink up, there's a good chap and in a moment you'll be fast asleep.

             (CONSCIENCE *drinks. It has an almost instant effect*)

             While it's taking effect, let me have another look at those other tablets you keep referring to.

CONSCIENCE   (*Drugged*) The commandments? They're just here...

MAN   Don't worry, I can reach them. Have you a pen or a chisel?

CONSCIENCE   Whuhnah floobnig dishtapaaahh... (*Snores*)

MAN   It's alright. There's one here. Just to make a few amendments. Yes, that's right, the Ten Amendments. (*He reads each commandment and then writes in his amendments, which are italicised*) 'I am the Lord your God. You shall have no other gods before me'...*for a good half hour at Christmas and Easter*. 'You shall not make for yourself any idol'...*various exemptions include: income, salary, pay rises or anything to do with personal finances*. 'You shall not take the name of the Lord your God in vain'...*except*

154

when you fall over and smash something really valuable. 'Remember the Sabbath day to keep it holy'...*to keep it wholly... free until the golf club fixture list is announced.* 'Honour your father and mother'...*until they become impossibly senile.* 'You shall not kill'...*your friends...without a jolly good motive anyway.* 'You shall not commit adultery'... *unless you can convince yourself that it really is true love this time.*

CONSCIENCE   (*Snoring deeply*)

MAN   Goodnight, Conscience. 'You shall not steal'...*it's so demeaning—and really sharp businessmen never call it that.* 'You shall not tell lies'...*if being economical with the truth can achieve the same results.* 'You shall not covet'...*but a rising standard of living will certainly give you confidence with the neighbours.* There we are. That's ironed out a few wrinkles. Fitter, trimmer and ready for the twenty-first century. Sleep well, Conscience.

In Cash Terms

YOUNG MAN
YOUNG WOMAN

If a society's values are judged by the extent to which the things it prizes most invade its language, then it is easy to see why money and materialism are the gods of our age in the West. The vocabulary of banking and commerce is vast. It has wormed its way into almost every area of thought and conversation; into metaphor, 'figures' of speech, even intimate 'exchange' between lovers. As governments put economic issues at the pinnacle of their achievements, how can we escape this pervasive reinforcement that money matters above everything?

Children of Thatcher's Britain seem to have had a particularly concentrated dose of this evil distortion of truth. Here are two of them in a silly sketch which exaggerates the point through a torrent of dreadful puns, made palatable only because of the satisfying levels of laughter they seem to provoke in performance.

(A YOUNG MAN *and a* YOUNG WOMAN *are working away in front of their screens in a money market. They tap away and make frantic deals over the telephone until the bell goes for the end of the day's trading. There is a slight pause. The* MAN *turns to the* WOMAN*)*

MAN   Whoof! Aaaah! *(He yawns and stretches with relief)* That's it, then for this week.

WOMAN   Yeah. Not bad, eh?

MAN   The weekend!

(Pause)

Give us a quid.

WOMAN   Not here, no.

MAN   *(Trying to embrace her)* Come on, just a quid. For me.

WOMAN   Somebody might be looking.

MAN   So? We can afford that. What's wrong?

WOMAN   *(Breaking away from him)* It's just that you're so fiscal.

MAN   Yeah, I'm sorry. It's my base rate. I'm no good with words. It comes from being brought up in a bank.

(Pause)

I was wondering if you would mind, well,...I don't really know how to put this.

WOMAN   What?

MAN   I was wondering if you would, well, think about investing our futures market with me...to coin a phrase?

WOMAN   Are we talking a long-term investment?

MAN	Of course. To be my finance. Yeah.
WOMAN	It's a deal.
MAN	That's capital!
WOMAN	I'm going into the red. I'm so happy, I could liquidate. (*She becomes weepy*)
MAN	So could I, only I don't find it quite so easy to float in public like that. Here, use my chequebook.

(*He hands it to her and she dries her eyes*)

WOMAN	Thank you.
MAN	Don't...er...don't cry on my account. Sorry. That was a terrible pun. Bit cheap. But darling, you realise we could be in business in three months. I'll make all the arrangements.
WOMAN	You're so dear. All I am is due to you.
MAN	No, no. Everything IOU.

(*They are about to kiss*)

WOMAN	(*Turning away*) You must have a mint.
MAN	Oh.

(*A little taken aback, he rummages in his pocket for some mints*)

WOMAN	There's something I ought to tell you. A loan. This might come as a shock. I saw my accountant last week.
MAN	(*Alarmed*) What, you don't mean–? You're not overdrawn?!

(*She nods*)

Oh, NO!! Are you sure? It's not just speculation? When did you find out?

WOMAN   Last week. The transaction was positive.

MAN   What did they say?

WOMAN   I'm already six weeks in arrears.

MAN   Debit! Debit! Debit! This could ruin us! Why didn't you tell me?

WOMAN   You're so uncommercial, there's never any exchange!

MAN   There'll be a lump sum soon. Inflation! People will start to make statements.

WOMAN   It's the price we have to pay.

MAN   That's rich coming from you. You told me you were insured!

WOMAN   Nothing's one hundred per cent confident, you know that. You have to make allowances.

MAN   Yeah, I'm sorry. I'm sorry. I've been an absolute rebate. Can you ever reimburse me?

WOMAN   Of course I can.

MAN   After all, we really subsidise each other don't we?

WOMAN   Without recession.

(*Pause*)

MAN   Oh,...Penny!

WOMAN   Oh,...Franc!

(*They embrace in front of an unbelievable sunset, to surging orchestral music, as the lights fade*)

Smothers Day

MRS ZEBEDEE
MR ZEBEDEE

In Matthew's Gospel (chapter 20, verse 20) the story is told of how the mother of the disciples James and John came and made them kneel before Jesus to beg positions of the highest honour in the future kingdom. It may not have been the case, but the mother appears to be the driving force behind this rather painfully amusing scene. It's not an entirely unnatural instinct to wish for preferment for one's children, nor is it surprising that it got up the noses of the other disciples (whose mothers were presumably not around to apply similar pressure on their behalf).

While Mother's day is an appropriate occasion for us all, as children, to express gratitude to our mothers or to celebrate Mother Church, it can also be helpful to some of us as parents to remember our responsibility to release our children into independence and maturity. All children are a gift from God—not ours to dominate or to continue to smother with the warm eiderdown of our own needs and feelings. Murray Watts tells this anecdote in *Bats in the Belfry*:

A mother was convinced that her wayward son would become a Christian. She lost no opportunity in telling him that one day he would come to the faith. She pleaded with him to mend his ways, to see the light; she sent him little cards with Bible verses on, spiritual books, tapes of powerful sermons, all to no avail. One day, she fell on her knees and prayed fervently that God would totally remove the obstacle to her son's conversion. There was a blinding flash and she vanished.

(*The Zebedees are at home.* MRS ZEBEDEE *is busy cleaning shoes, her husband is hovering behind her.*)

MOTHER   Well?

FATHER   Well, what?

MOTHER   Did you speak to him?

FATHER   Yes, I spoke to him.

MOTHER   Well, what did he say?

FATHER   …um…well…um…erm…

MOTHER   Sounds fascinating. Did he say anything else?

FATHER   Oh, yes.

MOTHER   Zebedee!! Did you speak to him about the boys?

FATHER   Well, I…um…in a way…yes…I, um…

MOTHER   So what did he say?

FATHER   Well, he said, 'Blessed are the meek'.

MOTHER   The meek! Typical! And who might they be? Do we know them? I've not seen them at any of the meetings.

FATHER   Well, I think he meant…

MOTHER   Did he say why?

FATHER   Why what, dear?

MOTHER   Why the *meek* should be so blessed all of a sudden? Our boys have been his closest friends for years! Never mind the meek! James and John have followed him all around the country. Though goodness knows who's been doing their laundry. I have given the best years of my life to get those

162

	boys started. And I am not about to stand by and see it all thrown away, even if you are!
FATHER	I taught them to fish.
MOTHER	Fish! Huh! The only thing those two are likely to catch in your boat is lumbago. They were never going to be interested in fishing. I could see that. And I can't say I blame them. You can't get rid of the smell. (*She recoils from the shoe she is trying to clean*) How many fishermen have you ever seen running the country?
FATHER	They wouldn't have the time, dear.
MOTHER	We've got to think of the future. Surprising as it may be in this family, those boys are intelligent. They're potential leaders. They deserve a good position.
FATHER	He said they would inherit the earth.
MOTHER	Well, that's *something*!
FATHER	No. The *meek*. The meek will inherit the earth.
MOTHER	I knew I shouldn't have left this to you. You've no idea. No idea at all. Do you realise who this Jesus is? That boy is going places. When he becomes king, they'll all come crawling out of the woodwork. Oh, yes. There'll be Mrs Maxwell, Mrs Oppenheimer and the Grades...talk about ideas above your station! And that Nathanael's mother. They'll all be trying to make out that they've supported him from the beginning. Trying to jump the queue. Well, I've gone along with this religious thing. It's been hard but I've done it. There

are some good jobs in religion, so we need to get this thing cleared up now, before the bunfight starts. Of course, you've wasted the first opportunity, haven't you? I should have spoken to Jesus myself. He'd have understood. He's a good boy. Always been very good to his mother. Not like our two. They never drop in here...even when they have to pass the door.

FATHER   James comes once a week when he's home.

MOTHER   It's like an appointment. One day they'll realise. They'll realise how much they owe their mother. I've had to push for everything. One day they'll be very grateful.

FATHER   They might be very embarrassed.

MOTHER   Nonsense! Those boys? Embarrassed by their mother? Embarrassed by their shilly-shallying father more like. I shall have to go and apologise for you. I shall come straight to the point. I shall ask for a full clarification of the prospects for James and John *and* I shall get a straight answer.

(*She begins to leave*)

FATHER   (*To himself*) It's no wonder they call them the Sons of Thunder.

MOTHER   What's that you say?

FATHER   Nothing, dear.

P.S. The authors wish it to be clear that any resemblance within this piece to persons close to them is entirely accidental and they also wish to be clear that they have ordered large quantities of flowers and chocolates to ease any misunderstanding.

Moving Molehills

MR PIMPLET, a man suffering from a serious loss of faith
NURSE
MR KILMORE-SLICE, a surgeon
ANAESTHETIST

Faith is an attribute that all human beings exercise
constantly in every day life. Chairs, going to sleep,
watching television: all require some degree of faith,
built up through natural experience. Why then, do so
many people find the concept of faith so strange when
it is exercised within the spiritual dimension? The
Bible describes spiritual faith as 'assurance' and 'con-
viction' about things we cannot see. Like any muscle,
this faith will atrophy if it is not exercised. It does not
seem unreasonable, therefore, to invite people who
already 'live by faith' in the natural world, to develop
the same gift within the spiritual one. This sketch
might be useful in starting that process. It illustrates
the level of faith which operates within, for example,
the ordinary life of a hospital every moment of the day
and night.

(MR PIMPLET, *dressed in pyjamas and dressing gown, waits anxiously in an operating theatre*)

MR PIMPLET   Nurse! (*Pause*) Nurse!

(*After a while a* NURSE *breezes in cheerfully*)

NURSE   Right then, Mr Pimplet, it's our Appendectomy Day today, isn't it?

MR PIMPLET   I'm not at all sure about this you know.

NURSE   Appendectomy? Oh, that's just a little technical word we use for chopping out your gibblies and sewing you back together again. Have you moved your bowels this morning?

MR PIMPLET   I'm not at all sure about going through with this, nurse. And my bowels have been in almost constant motion, thank you very much.

NURSE   Jolly good. Mr Kilmore-Slice did eighteen appendectomies yesterday and a by-pass. It's all quite routine.

MR PIMPLET   Not for me it isn't.

NURSE   Pop your jim-jams off then and let's get ready for surgeon, shall we?

MR PIMPLET   Now look here, Miss, I go to considerable lengths to ensure that my 'jim-jams' never sag an inch, let alone pop off! (*He reveals a sturdy pair of braces holding up his pyjama bottoms*)

NURSE   Oh my goodness! Look at the state of those! Still, better safe than sorry, eh?

166

MR PIMPLET	(*Lowering his voice*) One is never safe. I mean, how do I know these *braces* won't suddenly pop off? I take full precautions.
NURSE	Well, I'm sure that's very sensible of you.
	(*The* SURGEON *and the* ANAESTHETIST *enter briskly. They are both masked*)
SURGEON	Still wearing those ridiculous braces are we, Mr Pimplet? Well, come on, onto the operating table please.
MR PIMPLET	I prefer to stand. In case it collapses.
SURGEON	Oh really? Perhaps you'd also care for a bottle of the house red and a flamenco dancer while we do the operation? Now, come on, pop yourself up here.
MR PIMPLET	It's always *popping* with you people, isn't it?
ANAESTHETIST	There's absolutely nothing to worry about, Mr Pimplet. You can have complete faith in Mr Kilmore-Slice.
NURSE	He could do it with his eyes shut, he's done that many.
MR PIMPLET	With his eyes shut!?
ANAESTHETIST	He's very experienced.
	(*They manoeuvre* MR PIMPLET *on to the table*)
MR PIMPLET	How would I know? You could be telling me a whopper?

NURSE	Just lie back, nice and comfy.
MR PIMPLET	I mean, has he ever taken my appendix out before?
ANAESTHETIST	(*Busy with his preparations*) Of course not.
MR PIMPLET	Well, there you are you see! He's an absolute beginner as far as I'm concerned!...Fumbling his way through the uncharted layers of my stomach wall with a dessert spoon and a carving knife!
NURSE	Try to breathe normally.
MR PIMPLET	A fine state of affairs, that is!
SURGEON	Do you want to get better, or do you want to die of peritonitis, Mr Pimplet?
MR PIMPLET	I wouldn't let a total stranger cut my toenails.
SURGEON	Just exercise a little faith, Mr Pimplet. (*Three masked faces close in.*)
MR PIMPLET	Wait! Couldn't *I* do it? I'm sure I could have a go. (*Masks down.*)
SURGEON	I'm not sure we're entirely mentally stable, are we, Mr Pimplet? Here you have a qualified team of hospital staff with absolute faith in their ability to complete a simple operation and you want them to naff off to the canteen, leaving you to, shall we say, 'experiment' with a scalpel in your lower abdomen.

MR PIMPLET   You could give me a few tips.

              (*The* ANAESTHETIST *advances with a chloroform mask*)

              What's that he's holding?

ANAESTHETIST Your anaesthetic. It's chloroform.

MR PIMPLET   Well are you sure?! Did you check it? What was on the bottle?

ANAESTHETIST A big label marked 'Chloroform'.

MR PIMPLET   (*Seizing the bottle*) Well you can't trust labels! (*Sniffs hard*) You can't trust anything these days!

              (*The* SURGEON *silently counts to five on his fingers. Abruptly,* MR PIMPLET *passes out into the arms of the* SURGEON.)

SURGEON   Oh, I think you'll find you can, Mr Pimplet.

              (*The* NURSE *tosses him a scalpel, which he catches deftly*)

              Cut!

              (*They all freeze*)

The Wisdom and Folly Rap

RAPPER
WISEMAN, a mime
FOOL, a mime

This piece began life as a collection of verses from the Psalms, Ecclesiastes and Proverbs. In our first book, *Time To Act* (pub. Hodder & Stoughton), these verses were strung together as a continuous narration, illustrated in mime theatre by a WISEMAN and a FOOL. (A look back at this may suggest ideas for action.) Now, with the inexorable march of time, it appears as rap. This should still be choreographed into a sequence of physical theatre, using the same archetypal characters. Here and there, action has been suggested, mainly to elucidate the sense, rather than to limit your own creativity! You might also experiment with interchanging voices and various cartoon sound effects. The final line is deliberately two beats short to create a sudden ending. This is preceded by an unspoken line of four clear beats on the drum after which the last four words are delivered in silence.

(A fast rapping rhythm is established)

Consider wisdom, folly too
The difference should be plain to you.
Wisdom's light is clear as day
The fool goes stumbling on his way.
Yet I perceive again and again,
That one fate comes to each of them.

(Both WISEMAN *and* FOOL *collapse with heart failure)*

(As the WISEMAN*)* A nagging voice inside me said:
'Both wise and foolish end up dead.'
So that is where the puzzle lies—
No great incentive to be *wise*.

So tell me where true wisdom's found?
Not in knowledge, search around.
Knowledge gets us all puffed up *(The* FOOL *is inflated)*
And up and up and up and up!
Too much wind and you'll erupt.

(The FOOL *erupts)*

A fool has money in his hand
To buy all wisdom in the land.
But what's the use of purchasin'?
He has no *mind* to put it in.
One man pretends to be so rich,
Yet he has nothing—not a stitch.
Another seems to be so poor,
But has such hidden wealth in store.

(The WISEMAN *looks up to see treasure in heaven)*

So where on earth is wisdom found?
Where is the source? Just check the ground.
God looks from heaven upon us all,
Sees everything from wall to wall.
He understands the way to it.
He saw, declared, established it.

So fear of God is where it starts.
From evil ways we must depart.

Do justice, kindness, truth to tell.
Walk humbly with your God as well.
Do justice, kindness, truth to tell.
Walk humbly with your God as well.
The fool he says within his heart
(*beat, beat, beat, beat, stop*) 'There is no God.'

Judge Not

HIGH-COURT JUDGE
ANGEL
SAINT

Keeping on the right side of the law, even embodying
the law itself in society's terms, will be of little value
when each of us comes before the judgement seat of
God. There, only the mercy of God and the righteous-
ness we inherit as his children will count for anything.
This sketch asks us to face the sins of our hearts rather
than take confidence from an outward social morality.
Many of us live in cultures which retain the gloss of
Christian standards, but which avoid the heart of the
problem—the human heart.

(*A HIGH COURT JUDGE arrives in full robes and wig outside the gates of heaven, where an ANGEL is on duty*)

JUDGE Ooohff! That was quick. Not as much pain as the doctors thought there might be. (*He looks around*) Now, where are we? Ah, that's it.

(*He heads for a door marked 'HEAVEN'*)

ANGEL Er, would you mind holding on a moment, please, sir?

JUDGE Ah, hullo. I'm Lord Chief Justice Bul–

ANGEL That's right.

JUDGE Oh, you already know. That's good.

ANGEL Yes, we've been trying to get in touch for a while now.

JUDGE I imagine you have, yes.

(*Pause. He looks at the door*)

Mustn't be too hasty, I suppose.

ANGEL No, sir. Your case is being prepared right now.

JUDGE Case, eh?

ANGEL What was it in the end?

JUDGE Oh, heart attack. Yes. Too much Beaujolais and too many (*The ANGEL chimes in with him*) cream doughnuts.

(*Pause*)

Bit silly, really. Still, all over and done with now, eh?

ANGEL In one sense.

JUDGE Phase one completed. (*Pause*) This is some

174

kind of registration procedure, is it? Clearing up any loose ends. Not that there will be many of those, I fancy. (*Musing*) Yes, yes, forty-eight years at the top, upholding the law. It's quite something, really. Sending them down for goodness knows how long. 'If in doubt, hang 'em!' That's what I used to say. (*He chuckles alone*) It was a kind of joke I was famous for at the Bailey.

(*A SAINT enters with some papers for the ANGEL to check. The JUDGE recognises him*)

Good Lord!!

SAINT   No, sir. But He will be with you in a moment. (*To the angel*) Won't be long now, mate, but there's a fair bit to check through.

(*He leaves*)

JUDGE   Do you realise who that was?! Well, bless my soul, I gave that man thirty years for armed robbery.

ANGEL   Really. And now he's got eternal life. Well, well.

JUDGE   (*Laughing*) Eternal *Life*, yes! That's more like it. (*Pulls out fob watch*) Look, I know how long these legal things can take but I should have thought it would be quite straightforward. Tick them off: Armed Robbery? No. Arson? No. Murder? No. Mind you, there are a lot of charitable donations and one thing and another, so that could take time. Come on, come on.

(SAINT *re-enters*)

SAINT   (*Handing more papers to the angel*) Could you get this list checked for me? Ta.

JUDGE   I suppose you do know who you are, do you?

SAINT   Who me?

JUDGE   Yes. Semtex Sid.

SAINT   That's right. An' you'll be Basher Bulstrode, won't yer? Back in a tick.

(*He goes out*)

ANGEL   I wonder if you would mind checking this for me, sir? Does this list mean anything to you?

JUDGE   What's all this, then? (*Gets out his spectacles*) 'Covetousness, Lust, Wrath, (*Unconsciously pronouncing it to rhyme with wrath*) Sloth...er, (*correcting himself*) Sloth, Avarice, Gluttony, Pride.' It's your seven deadlies, I'd say, not that they mean very much these days. Now, if you'd put them down as: Theft, Rape, Murder, Loitering, Tax-dodging and Belching in Court, I'd be on home ground and well in the clear too I might add.

ANGEL   And Pride?

JUDGE   Ooh, no, not that one. That's not an offence any more. You can't get people for pride these days. If you could, we'd have half the country in the dock! I expect you'll find that Satan was the last person to get sent down for pride. (*He chuckles*)

(*Semtex Sid has re-entered in time to overhear the last remark*)

SAINT   No, mate. I'm afraid he wasn't.

JUDGE   What's that?

176

ANGEL   These are the crimes that are of particular interest to the Eternal Judge, you see.

JUDGE   What, you mean the Covetousness, Pride and...so forth?

(*The* ANGEL *nods. There is a short pause*)

ANGEL   We're still using the old list.

JUDGE   Really? Oh dear, dear, dear. I wish I'd known. Nobody told me. I thought I'd done rather well. Oh dear. Rather gone and prepared the wrong brief, you see.

(*Pause*)

SAINT   (*Gently*) The, er...'Good Lord' will see you now.

(*He shows the* JUDGE *the way*)

JUDGE   Oh dear, dear, dear.

APPENDIX ONE
The Stratford End

ANGUS, a director at the Royal Shakespeare Company
PETER, an actor
OLIVIA, an actor
BRIAN, a theatre advertising consultant

In the brave new world full of budgets and bankers, to what lengths will we be driven to preserve our souls and our culture? Disturbingly, this sketch may not prove to be as absurd as it seems. And what is tragedy anyway?

(*Two of the actors of the Royal Shakespeare Company,* PETER *and* OLIVIA, *are onstage waiting for rehearsals to begin.* BRIAN, *an accountant, is also present.* ANGUS, *the director, enters*)

ANGUS Thanks for coming in early everybody. Problems I'm afraid. I have to tell you that the whole Stratford season is now in jeopardy.

PETER (*To* OLIVIA) Working abroad, eh?

ANGUS It's not that funny actually, Peter. The government has just withdrawn all our support for the coming year in favour of what they call a Curtailed Revenue Arts Sponsorship Scheme. The Minister was on the phone to me at the week-end.

PETER C.R.A.S.S. That sounds typical.

ANGUS Yes, it basically means that we are staring a two million pound deficit in the face by the end of 1995, forcing us to look to the private sector. However, the good news is that Brian Martin here has agreed to become our new Theatre Advertising Consultant and he has already come up with a number of deals to save the current production of Mac–...the Scottish play. (*Introducing them*) Brian, Olivia, Olivia, Brian. Peter Edgar who's playing...er...the Scottish king.

OLIVIA Hello.

BRIAN Hi!

PETER Welcome.

BRIAN Thank you.

ANGUS Brian comes with an excellent track-record in sponsorship, particularly in sport. In fact, I think your only failure was the *Lean Cuisine* World Darts Championship, which fell through at the last minute.

BRIAN   It was actually one of the contestants who fell through...but anyway, the deal collapsed due to loss of consumer confidence.

ANGUS   The game is, of course, all about marrying the right product with the right event.

BRIAN   Yes indeed. You'll probably remember the fuss earlier this year over the Peaudouce Football League Cup, which was doomed from the moment the players refused to wear the gear in the Wembley final.

ANGUS   Still, interesting choice of costume won't be such a problem with theatre.

BRIAN   Exactly. Hence the reference to the Levi 501s and medical support tights worn by King Duncan when he arrives at Dunsinane. Page 32 in my script.

PETER   What??!!

ANGUS   Let's not jump the gun, Brian. I think we need to help our leading actors to work carefully and sensibly through the various textual alterations you've come up with before we broach them with the rest of the cast. Over to you then, Brian, to guide us through...calculator in hand!

BRIAN   Thank you. I'm sure I can count on your cooperation in giving increased commercial edge to our work.

OLIVIA Rising to the artistic legacy of Thatcherism, Brian.

BRIAN   Precisely. In cutting costs, some doubling will be necessary and Angus has also agreed to help out. (*Handing out scripts*) Page one then. Could you read in for all three witches. As we go through scene by scene, you will see how I am suggesting that we establish private sponsorship for each Act. So, lights up on the three witches. Off you go.

PETER   When shall we three meet again?
In thunder, lightning or in rain?

OLIVIA   When the hurly...

BRIAN   (*From out front*) A big logo for the Scottish Widows Association is coming up behind you, but don't worry about that, just keep improvising.

OLIVIA   When the battle's lost and won.

ANGUS   A sailor's wife had chestnuts in her lap
And mounch'd and mounch'd and mounch'd.

OLIVIA   Give me, quoth I (*All sing and dance together a popular jingle about potato crisps*) 'Cos they've got Walkers on the packet!'

PETER   Oh really!

BRIAN   (*Out front*) Don't let's have a flood of comments at this stage, Peter. Let's just do it and quibble over the details later. Olivia, can you try your speech for Lady Macbeth on 29...the raven himself...? And Peter, could you have a peep at your soliloquy on 48?

OLIVIA   Erm...The raven himself is hoarse
That croaks the fatal entrance of Duncan
Under my battlements. Come you Aussies

that tend on Castlemaine, four X me here,
And fill me...Brian, is that a deleted expletive
on line 41? (*Pause*) I'm not quite sure what she
is talking about here.

BRIAN   (*Out front*) Australian lager.

OLIVIA   Lager???

BRIAN   Yes. Castlemaine four X, it's a popular brand
of lager.

OLIVIA   Is there some motivation for invoking Aus-
tralians at this point?

BRIAN   (*After a short silence*) Carry on!

OLIVIA   And fill me from the crown to the toe, top-full
of amber nectar.

BRIAN   Lovely. We can discuss the accent later, but
that's fine.

PETER   (*Taking* ANGUS *on one side*) This has got to be a
joke. Who is this berk?

ANGUS   It isn't a joke, Peter. This is government pol-
icy.

PETER   Well, look at this! There is no way I am going
out there saying this garbage. (*Passes* ANGUS
his next speech) This is obscene prostitution!

BRIAN   What's the problem?

ANGUS   Peter's just having a few thoughts about his
soliloquy.

PETER   (*To* BRIAN) Now look here, I absolutely refuse
to go out there and say 'Is this a Wilkinson
stainless steel cutlery service for six I see
before me? The beautiful craftsman-made,

182

ivory-look handles towards my hand!!' No matter what the government says.

BRIAN   We can forget the set then.

OLIVIA   What do you mean?

ANGUS   Wilkinson's are providing all the metalwork.

BRIAN   (*Still out front*) Let's not worry unduly at this stage, Peter, as we may have to change the line in any case.

PETER   Why?

BRIAN   Wilkinson's are not too happy about their products being used to murder people, especially a king.

OLIVIA   What do we do then? Shave him to death?

(*Pause*)

ANGUS   Shall we go on to the Porter scene, Brian?

BRIAN   Okay. There are a number of possibilities here. Angus, let me take you through the stage directions. (ANGUS *acts*) There's a loud banging in the wings. The Porter staggers on, completely drunk and falls over. Then, Peter, you come in with your line.

PETER   I bet he drinks Carling Black Label.

BRIAN   Which I think is fair enough considering this scene is being paid for by a brand of alcohol-free beer.

PETER   This is outrageous! This is the Royal Shakespeare Company for goodness sake!

ANGUS   (*From where he is lying on the floor*) Peter, I sympathise and believe me, we don't want to recast at this stage. By the way, as from last Friday, we are now the—what are we, Brian?

BRIAN   The Royal Flora Margarine Company.

ANGUS   (PETER *tries to attack* BRIAN. ANGUS *restrains him*) Peter! Peter! Please! Just sit down with some coffee while Olivia does the sleep-walking scene. Brian, could you read in for Peter in this next bit?

BRIAN   Certainly.

OLIVIA   We've got to give this a try, Peter.

BRIAN   That's the spirit.

(OLIVIA *begins acting; sleepwalking and rubbing her hands*)

BRIAN   What is it she does now? Look how she rubs her hands.

ANGUS   It is an accustomed action with her, to seem thus washing her hands. I have known her continue in this a quarter of an hour.

OLIVIA   Yet here's a spot.

BRIAN   Mrs Macbeth has been using an ordinary detergent for many years.

OLIVIA   Out damned spot! Out I say!

ANGUS   We invited her to try washing her left hand in a new biological brand, with a tough action to combat really persistent stains.

BRIAN   While still continuing to wash her right hand in the ordinary detergent.

OLIVIA   (*Raising her right hand*) Here's the smell of blood still: all the perfumes of Arabia will not

184

	sweeten this little hand. But... (*Raising the left one*) Oh! Oh! Oh!
ANGUS	Pleased with the results, Mrs Macbeth?
OLIVIA	Remarkable. The bloodstains have completely disappeared, leaving my hand soft and fragrant.
BRIAN	Care to name it for us?
OLIVIA	New Forensic Bold. Only £4.99 for an economy packet.
ANGUS	Well done. What do you think Peter? Nicely blended in, wasn't it? (PETER *is in despair, head in hands*) Fine.
OLIVIA	Doesn't it rather upset the plot?
ANGUS	I don't think anyone will notice, quite frankly. They're so used to commercial breaks on television.
BRIAN	Just Peter's death scene, then.
OLIVIA	He looks about ready for it.
ANGUS	(*Speaking softly and gently to him*) Peter, we've just got to pay for the last few pages, but this doesn't involve you in any new bits of dialogue. Play that final confrontation with Macduff with all your usual skill and courage.
	(PETER *is led out like a lamb to the slaughter*)
PETER	(*Quietly*) I hate you, Angus.
ANGUS	Then use it. Use that hatred for Macbeth's last struggle.
BRIAN	Angus, remember Macduff is glorying in his one-up-manship here. He's gloating over

Macbeth because he knows that fate is on his side.

(*The lights focus on the two actors who speak in Scottish accents, their swords drawn*)

ANGUS   Turn hell-hound! Turn! Thou bloodlier villain
Than terms can give thee out!

PETER   Thou losest labour!
Let fall thy blade on vulnerable crests
I bear a charmed life; which must not yield
To one of woman born.

ANGUS   Despair thy charm
And let the angel whom thou still hast serv'd
Tell thee, Macduff was from his mother's womb
Untimely ripp'd. But think thou well on this
Commercial Union is thy safest armour
For we'll not make a crisis from a drama!

(*Stabs him*)

PETER   Accursed be the tongue that tells me so... (*He dies*)

APPENDIX TWO
The Riding Lights Membership Scheme

In order to save Riding Lights Theatre Company from the absurdities of the sketch in Appendix One, why not become a Member of Riding Lights and

BE PART OF THE VISION...

The vision of Riding Lights is:

- To provide high quality productions communicating a truthful understanding of life
- To reach a broad audience with work of lasting value
- To affirm the presence of Christ within professional theatre
- To reawaken a strong dramatic tradition within the Christian community

Over the past eighteen years, Riding Lights Theatre Company has grown from a small community project in York, into a significant UK touring company, bringing a wide range of innovative theatre productions to thousands of people each year as well as reaching a considerable international audience through occasional tours, radio broadcasts on the BBC World Service and through the widespread overseas sales of books such as this.

Riding Lights Theatre Company was formed when a group of professional actors and writers were given practical support by a local church with a radical approach to its role in the community. Initial finance came from the generosity of a few individuals with a clear calling to support the vital contribution that Christian artists can make to the character of our society. Since then Riding Lights has been a pioneer in reinstating theatre as a powerful means of Christian communication in a world dominated by the visual media.

Its early hallmarks of comedy and innovation caused it to be hailed as 'Christian theatre with a difference' (*Church of England Newspaper*, 1978). Concentrating on new writing and an ensemble style of theatre, the company's work has stretched far beyond the lightning biblical sketches for which it was originally famous; its productions have ranged across the theatrical board from street theatre to classic plays. Satirical revues have won awards at the Edinburgh International Festival, educational shows have been devised for schools, new full-length plays, sketches and musicals have been performed not only in some of the UK's premier theatres and on national television and radio, but in venues as diverse as universities, cathedrals, factories and prisons. Riding Lights has been on and through many different stages; many individual artists and technicians have played their part in its creative success; but also, most significantly, many other people have provided the ongoing practical support to keep this work and this vision alive during a time when so many other companies have disappeared.

The realities of funding such work took a new direction in 1992 with the launch of the *Riding Lights*

Membership Scheme, which in its first two years has been joined by over 800 people. In a way that would have been impossible without such enthusiastic and committed support, the company is gaining increasing independence from other funding bodies and the freedom to plan its programme prayerfully into the future. The support of members has brought about a resurgence of the primary vision of the company, outlined in the statement above. Working in three different spheres—community theatre, regional touring and mainstream productions, Riding Lights is reaching (at the time of this publication) a theatre audience of 180,000 people every year, many of whom would not go regularly to the theatre, let alone to church.

Within the first two years of running the Membership Scheme, many new developments have been realised. The Riding Lights Roughshod company, our community theatre operation based for weeks at a time on local churches around the country and serving multifarious venues from the sublime to the ridiculous, has become so well established that two Roughshod companies will soon be working simultaneously. In addition, there has been a highly successful regional tour of a play by Murray Watts, our first major prison tour, the commissioning of three new productions, eleven residential theatre courses, the creation of radio, television and video programmes, as well as the hosting of many theatre training days and workshops for churches and organisations nationwide. In 1992, Riding Lights received a Templeton UK Project Award 'for enabling audiences to hear the gospel gladly'. All of this work has been undergirded by the generous support of the Members of Riding Lights.

Time and time again the company has proved how effective theatre is in reaching the parts which other forms of Christian communication fail to reach. In the present climate of social fragmentation and the increasing isolation brought about by electronic media entertainment, the company's work is needed more than ever. We cannot do this on our own. We continue to seek a widening network of people contributing creatively, prayerfully and financially to establish the increased vision which we believe that God has given us. Can we invite you to become part of this vision?

The membership partnership brings to Riding Lights an informed, enthusiastic nucleus of support across the country, championing our cause in the community. Each supporter is a vital link with the needs of our audiences and a creative resource for new ideas. In return, we offer you a Membership card and information pack about the current state and programme of the company, a quarterly Members' Newsletter, advance booking opportunities at discounted prices for regional and mainstream productions, free participation in Days of Action Workshops and Members' seminars, the possibility of meeting with other members in your area for feedback sessions, prayer groups and backstage visits. We want our members to become as fully involved in the life of the company as they are able or would wish to be.

There is no fixed charge for membership. The only financial condition of membership is commitment to some regular contribution to the Riding Lights Trust (Registered Charity No. 507803) at whatever level is appropriate to you. No contribution is too small or too large as long as it is regular. Initially, we have been seeking to find 2,500 members whose contribution might average £5.00 per month. With this level of support, Riding Lights would be able to fulfill its target of two Roughshod companies, two regional tours of new plays and two mainstream productions each year.

If you are interested in becoming a Member of Riding Lights, or in receiving further information, please write care of 'Divine Comedies', P.O. Box 223, York, YO1 1GW.

We believe that God is giving us the faith and the means to respond to a passage in Isaiah that has propelled us forward since 1992:

> 'Enlarge the place of your tent, stretch your curtains wide. Do not hold back; lengthen your cords and strengthen your stakes. For you will spread abroad to the right and to the left and your descendants will people the desolate cities.'

With your help we will continue to develop this vision.

Paul Burbridge (Artistic Director) and Murray Watts (Associate Director), Riding Lights Theatre Company, September 1994.